# MUDWORKS

# MUDWORKS

## Creative Clay, Dough, and Modeling Experiences

MaryAnn F. Kohl

illustrations
Kathleen Kerr

BRIGHT IDEAS FOR
LEARNING CENTERS

Bright Ring
Publishing

## CREDITS

**Typography:** Trish Lemon, Towner Printing, Inc.
**Illustrations:** Kathleen Kerr
**Cover Photography:** Rod del Pozo/Pyramid
**Cover Design:** MaryAnn and Michael Kohl
**Hands Model:** Rachel Kohl

ISBN 0-935607-02-1
Library of Congress Catalog Card Number: 88-92897
Copyright © 1989 MaryAnn F. Kohl

Manufactured in the United States of America

10   9   8   7   6

Distributed by
GRYPHON HOUSE, INC.
3706 Otis Street     P.O. Box 275
Mt. Rainier, MD 20712

Published by
BRIGHT RING PUBLISHING
P.O. Box 5768
Bellingham, WA 98227

### Publisher's Cataloging in Publication
*(Prepared by Quality Books Inc.)*

Kohl, Mary Ann F.
   Mudworks : creative clay, dough, and modeling experiences / MaryAnn F. Kohl ; illustrations, Kathleen Kerr. --
   p.  cm. -- (Bright ideas for learning centers)
   Includes bibliographical references and index.
   ISBN 0-935607-02-1
   1. Handicraft--Juvenile literature.   2. Modeling--Juvenile literature.   I. Kerr, Kathleen. II. Title. III. Series: Kohl, Mary Ann F. Bright ideas for learning centers.

TT160                    745.5
                              88-92897
                              MARC

FOR BETTER OR FOR WORSE © 1988 Universal Press Syndicate
Reprinted with permission. All rights reserved.

# ACKNOWLEDGEMENTS

I would like to thank the many people who have made this book possible, who have worked towards encouraging children's creativity, and who have cared about and encouraged me throughout the publication of this book.

I am especially grateful to the following people who have helped with book production:
to Kathleen Kerr for her delightful artwork, to Trish Lemon who has been more than a typographer and is a friend, to Rod del Pozo for his wonderful photography, to the people of Gryphon House (Larry Rood, Sarabeth Goodwin, Jean Racine) for advice in publishing, to Merry Reavis and Pat George for proofing, to Ray Sevin of Bookcrafters for patient manufacturing advice, and to Bonnie Stafford for friendship and skill in indexing.

To those friends and teaching peers who have encouraged me and supported me, I thank you:
Patricia Asmundson, Kristy Champagne, Judy McCoy, Ellen Challenger, Jack Groom, Kathy Dorr, and Kris Grinstad.

And to my family, I thank you for your input in book design and content, experimentation in projects, and support in all aspects of publishing. You have helped to make the goal of writing and publishing possible:
Michael Kohl, Hannah Kohl, and Megan Kohl

## DEDICATION

In loving memory of my parents,
John Ross and Betty Louise Faubion

# TABLE OF CONTENTS

*"Let me be the one
to do what is done."*
— Robert Frost

## FOREWORD

The creative modeling experiences in this book were developed and compiled
for independent expression by children of all ages. Each recipe and activity
needs no adult model to copy; children simply explore and create from the
materials at hand. The outcome of each experience is bounded only by the
child's imagination. Some projects will be lovely to look at, some lovely to taste,
and others lovely to have explored and nothing more. Children will need only to
please themselves.

# INTRODUCTION
for parents and teachers

MUDWORKS is a book of open-ended clay, dough, and other modeling art experiences. There is no right or wrong way for projects to turn out. Exploration and experimentation in sculpture, design, and play is encouraged for all ages. After children have explored and repeatedly experienced the modeling qualities of doughs and clays, they will begin to refine their work automatically and independently.

Young children may assist in preparation of doughs and clays with supervision. Older children will work more independently. The decision as to how much each child can handle safely and successfully is yours along with the child's.

Once modeling mixtures are prepared, freedom in exploration and experimentation will be encouraged and enjoyed. Adult models to copy are not necessary. But this is not to say adults should not join in and enjoy the art experiences too! Free-form designs, as opposed to perfect ''cookie-cutter'' products, are the goal of the projects in MUDWORKS.

Explore. Experiment. Create. Enjoy watching the creative sparkle of each child.

*note: all flours in MUDWORKS are non-self-rising wheat flour, unless otherwise stated. (bleached or unbleached all purpose flour)

t. = teaspoon
T. = Tablespoon

sealants include any of the following:
    glazes
    clear enamel
    polymers
    sprays
    laquers
    or nail polish

# THE SYMBOLS

Throughout MUDWORKS graphic symbols have been conveniently located in the upper page corner of each project or recipe to give you instant access to the qualities and use of each. These symbols will help with choosing those activities and recipes most suitable for you and the child.

For all dough and clay preparation, adult supervision should be considered, especially when cooking or baking is involved. The symbols below indicate things to consider during the *use* of the mixture, *rather than in the preparation.* Appropriate age suggestions are also based on the *use of the mixture, rather than the preparation.*

The following symbols are to be used *only as guidelines and are not mandatory.* Please judge the art experiences in MUDWORKS based on your knowledge of the children involved. Feel free to experiment and change the mixtures and their uses to your own artistic choice and pleasure.

 mixture needs no cooking *before use*

 mixture or art objects are edible only eat mixtures with this symbol

 mixture needs cooking *in preparation*

 caution suggested

 art objects can be baked for permanence

 adult supervision for all ages

 art objects can air dry

 age appropriate for *use* of mixture this is only a suggestion

# PLAYDOUGH
## chapter 1

The 37 recipes in this chapter are meant to be explored and enjoyed without definite outcomes. Each dough or clay has textures, smells, and modeling qualities unique to itself that require no planned results. Children explore and create freely. Many of the recipes give suggestions for variations to expand the enjoyment of the recipe after the child has had a chance to explore. Feel free to experiment and mix ideas from one page to another.

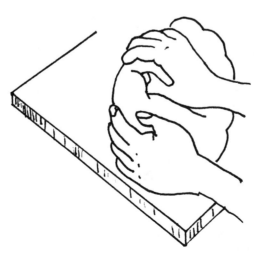

# SALTY FUNDOUGH

*nice consistency — good for young children*

**MATERIALS:**
1 cup flour
1 cup water
½ cup salt
2 t. cream of tartar
2 T. oil
pan

**PROCESS:**
1. mix all ingredients in pan
2. cook until thickened over low heat
3. cool
4. knead
5. explore dough freely

# SALT PLAYDOUGH

*excellent cooked dough*

## MATERIALS:

1 cup water
½ cup flour
1 cup salt

saucepan
wax paper, rolling pin
food coloring, optional
airtight container

## PROCESS:

1. mix all ingredients in saucepan
2. add food coloring if desired
3. stir over low heat
4. when thick and rubbery, remove from heat
5. spoon part of clay onto a floured sheet of wax paper
6. roll out
7. cut out or model objects
8. dry objects for a few days
9. store covered dough in airtight container to prevent drying

## VARIATIONS:

1. use straws to punch holes for hanging
2. glue sequins to clay
3. paint
4. make beads and string on yarn
5. make a clay bowl by rolling clay into coils
6. press macaroni into sides before clay hardens

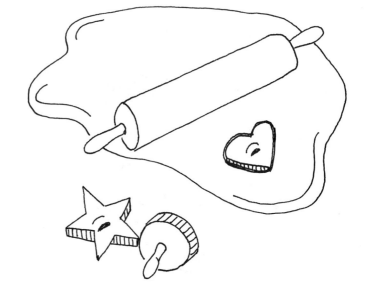

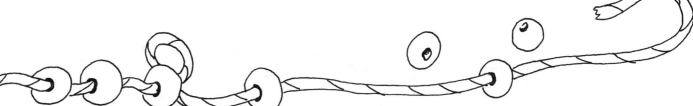

# PLAY CLAY

*pure white — hardens quickly*

## MATERIALS:
1 cup baking soda
½ cup cornstarch
⅔ cup warm water
food coloring or poster paints
shellac or clear nail polish
saucepan
board

## PROCESS:
1. mix baking soda and cornstarch in saucepan
2. add water and stir until smooth
3. over medium heat, boil and stir until like mashed potatoes
4. pour onto board to cool
5. knead when cool
6. for color, knead coloring into clay until blended
   or paint when finished
7. when dry, brush with shellac or nail polish

## HINTS:
1. makes 1½ cups, doubles well
2. hardens quickly
3. stores in airtight container for several weeks

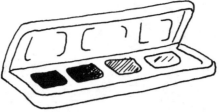

# CORNSTARCH DOUGH

*slightly grainy and white — keeps well*

**MATERIALS:**
½ cup salt
½ cup hot water
¼ cup cold water
½ cup cornstarch
pan
bowl
board

**PROCESS:**
1. mix salt and hot water and boil in pan
2. stir cold water into cornstarch in bowl
3. add cornstarch mixture to boiling water and stir
4. cook over low, stirring until like pie dough
5. remove and turn onto a board
6. when cool, knead until smooth
7. explore dough freely

**HINTS:**
1. texture is grainy
2. hardens in 1 to 2 days
3. is white
4. speed drying time in oven 200° for 1 hour
5. keeps a long time if stored in container

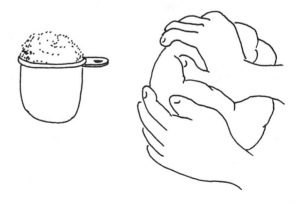

# FUNCLAY 1

*smooth, white dough — good for making animals*

## MATERIALS:
water colors, tempera paints, wax paper
1 cup salt
½ cup cornstarch
1 cup boiling water
pan
wet cloth

## PROCESS:
1. mix all ingredients in a pan
2. boil to a soft ball stage
3. knead on wax paper until dough-like
4. wrap in wet cloth to keep for a few days
5. by holding a lump of clay in hands, pull out the clay to make legs or arms and head and tail
6. let animals dry and then paint

## VARIATIONS:
1. make free-form designs
2. make ornaments for holidays or birthdays

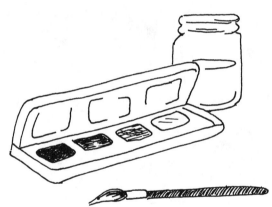

# FUNCLAY 2

## MATERIALS:

| | |
|---|---|
| 1 cup cornstarch | pan |
| 2 cups salt | bowl |
| 1⅓ cups cold water | spoon |
| paint | plastic bag |

## PROCESS:

1. put salt and ⅔ cup water in a pan and boil
2. mix cornstarch with remaining water in bowl and stir well
3. add salt mixture to cornstarch mixture in bowl
4. knead
5. model or mold clay and let dry several hours
6. paint when dry, if desired

## HINTS:

1. makes 3 cups
2. keep unused clay in a covered container, or plastic bag in refrigerator

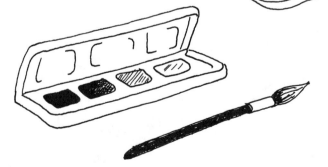

# SALTY OIL DOUGH 1

*children enjoy
kneading warm dough*

## MATERIALS:

½ cup flour      medium bowl
2 T. salt      saucepan
1 t. cream of tartar (optional)      spoon
⅓ cup water      jar with lid, or plastic wrap
1 t. cooking oil

## PROCESS:

1. measure the flour and salt into a bowl
2. add optional cream of tartar as a preservative
3. boil water in saucepan and pour into flour mixture
4. add oil
5. stir until mixed
   (dough will be sticky)
6. roll and squeeze warm dough in hands for 5 minutes
   (the longer it is handled, the nicer it gets)
7. model and explore as with any clay
8. store in airtight container or plastic wrap

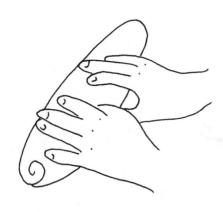

# SALTY OIL DOUGH 2

*very workable*

**MATERIALS:**
1 cup flour
1 T. vegetable oil
1 cup water
½ cup salt
2 t. cream of tartar
food coloring
saucepan
covered container
spoon

**PROCESS:**
1. heat all ingredients over low heat in saucepan, stirring until ball forms
2. knead
3. explore dough freely
4. store in covered container or plastic bag

# SAND MODELING

*molds or models beautifully — stonelike when dry*

## MATERIALS:
1 cup sand
½ cup cornstarch
1 t. alum
¾ cup hot water
food coloring (optional)
bowl
pan
airtight container

## PROCESS:
1. mix sand, cornstarch, and alum in bowl
2. add hot water, stirring vigorously
3. add food coloring if desired
4. cook over medium heat until thick in pan
5. cool
6. model or mold into objects
7. dry in sunshine for several days
8. store left over dough in airtight container

## HINTS:
1. makes 2 cups
2. grainy and stonelike
3. does not need shellac or varnish for protection

# SALT OIL ALUM DOUGH

*easily accepts experimental ingredients
such as sand, coffee, or glitter*

## MATERIALS:

2 cups water                    pan
½ cup salt                      spoon
food coloring
2 T. salad oil
2 T. alum
2 cups flour

## PROCESS:

1. boil water, salt, and food coloring in pan
2. remove from heat
3. add oil, alum and flour
4. while hot, mix and knead 5 minutes
5. explore and model dough freely

## VARIATIONS:

1. try adding a fragrance
2. try kneading in a texture such as coffee grounds, sawdust, vermiculite, or other grainy items

# SUGAR DOUGH

*sticky and fun*

### MATERIALS:
| | |
|---|---|
| 1 cup sugar | pan |
| 1 cup flour | spoon |
| 1 cup cold water | |
| 5 cups boiling water | |

### PROCESS:
1. mix sugar, flour, and cold water in pan
2. add boiling water and cook 5 minutes, stirring
3. cool
4. model and explore dough freely

### HINTS:
1. does not keep well
2. sticky and fun

# LINT MODELING

*unusual ingredients*
*molds well — a little like papier-mache*

**MATERIALS:**
3 cups dryer lint
2 cups cold or warm water
⅔ cup flour
3 drops oil of cloves
old newspapers
saucepan
box, bottle, balloon, or mold

**PROCESS:**
1. stir lint and water in a saucepan
2. add flour and stir to prevent lumps
3. add oil of cloves
4. cook over low and stir until mixture forms peaks
5. pour out and cool on newspapers
6. shape over boxes, bottles, balloons or press into a mold, or use like papier-mache (see Chapter 4)

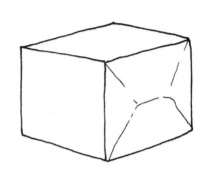

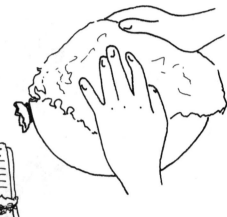

**HINTS:**
1. makes 4 cups
2. dries in 3 to 5 days
3. very hard, durable
4. dries smooth if pressed into a mold
5. dries rougher if shaped over an object

# BASIC ART DOUGH

*the best and easiest uncooked dough*

## MATERIALS:
4 cups flour
1 cup iodized salt
1¾ cups warm water
bowl

## PROCESS:
1. mix all ingredients in bowl
2. knead 10 minutes
3. model as with any clay
4. bake 300° until hard
5. or air dry for a few days

# BAKERS CLAY

*versatile, soft, pliable —
similar to Basic Art Dough*

## MATERIALS:
4 cups flour          1½ cups water          plastic bag
1 cup salt            bowl, spoon

## PROCESS:
1. mix salt in warm water until partially dissolved, then add to flour, or,
   mix flour and salt, then add water
2. mix with a spoon until the particles stick together, then
3. form a ball with your hands and knead 5 to 10 minutes
4. explore dough freely

## HINTS:
1. if a rolled coil splits, dough needs more kneading until coil holds together
2. if dough does not knead properly, add a few drops of water at a time and work until dough is satiny smooth
3. if dough is too moist, add flour (dough will be stiff)
4. keep ball of dough in a plastic bag or covered bowl and take out only what you need (use within 24 hours)

## VARIATIONS:
1. bake at 300° on cookie sheet for about 1 hour
2. let cool and paint, if desired
3. spray with clear varnish or fixative (finished pieces may be glued together)
4. can be baked at 250° 1 to 3 hours
5. half, double, or triple this recipe
   *hint:* measure carefully
6. glaze with egg white, evaporated milk, or mayonnaise before baking
7. color before shaping by mixing color with water

# OILY DOUGH 1

*easy, models well, keeps well*

**MATERIALS:**
3 cups flour
1 cup salt
3 T. oil
1 cup water
bowl

**PROCESS:**
1. mix flour and salt in bowl
2. stir in oil and water
3. add more water if necessary to form soft dough
4. explore dough freely

# OILY DOUGH 2

*good for young children —*
*very pliable*

**MATERIALS:**
3 cups flour
1 cup salt
1 T. oil
1 cup water with food coloring
bowl

**PROCESS:**
1. mix dry ingredients in bowl
2. add water and oil gradually
3. add more water if too stiff
4. add more flour if too sticky
5. model as with any dough

# SALT MODELING CLAY

*doubles well for large group projects*

## MATERIALS:
1 cup flour
½ cup salt
1 t. alum
⅓ to ½ cup water
food coloring (optional)
bowl
airtight container

## PROCESS:
1. combine flour, salt, and alum in bowl
2. add water a little at a time, and stir into flour
   *hint:* like pie-dough
3. knead until smooth
4. model as with any clay
5. let dry 2 to 3 days
   or, bake 1 to 2 hours at 200°

## HINTS:
1. will store in airtight container for a long time
2. food coloring can be added or kneaded into moist clay
3. different coloring can be added to divided portions
4. doubles well for large groups or projects

## VARIATIONS:
1. roll out and cut this clay
2. press designs into clay

# QUICK MODELING

*quick and easy —*
*makes a bright colored clay*

## MATERIALS:
1 cup cold water
1 cup salt
2 t. oil
3 cups flour
2 T. cornstarch
powdered paint or food coloring

## PROCESS:
1. mix the water, salt, oil and enough powdered paint to make a bright color
2. gradually work flour and cornstarch in until like bread dough
3. knead
4. model as with any clay

# OIL ALUM CLAY

*makes one cup — doubles well*

## MATERIALS:

¾ cup flour
½ cup salt
1½ t. alum
1½ t. vegetable oil
½ cup boiling water
food coloring

pan
bowl
spoon
airtight container

## PROCESS:

1. combine flour, salt, and alum in bowl
2. boil water in pan, add oil, and add to mixture in bowl
3. stir with spoon
4. add food coloring and knead until blended
5. explore dough freely

## HINTS:

1. makes 1 cup, so you may want to mix several doubles
2. dries hard overnight
3. store in jar with tight lid
4. will keep several months without refrigeration

## VARIATIONS:

1. make several batches of different colors
2. try adding scents

# SALT AND ALUM MODELING

*dries to extreme hardness and paints well*

**MATERIALS:**
1 cup flour
1 cup salt
1 rounded t. powdered alum
water
bowl
paint, optional

**PROCESS:**
1. add water slowly to first three ingredients in bowl
2. knead until clay-like
3. model as with any clay
4. dry to extreme hardness
5. paint, if desired

# EASY SALT DOUGH

*resembles Baker's Clay*

**MATERIALS:**
1½ cups flour
¾ cup salt
¾ cup water
bowl

**PROCESS:**
1. mix all ingredients in bowl
2. add more water if needed
3. knead into soft dough
4. model as with any dough

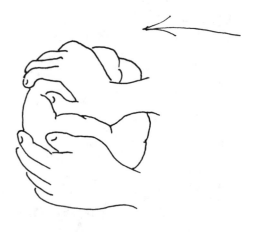

# OILY CLOUD DOUGH

*very oily, unique tactile experience*

**MATERIALS:**
1 cup oil
6 cups flour
food coloring
bowl
spoon

**PROCESS:**
1. mix oil, flour, and food coloring in bowl with spoon
2. knead
3. add more flour if needed
4. explore and use dough freely

**HINTS:**
1. dough is very oily
2. wear apron and wash hands with soap and water after using

# COFFEE DOUGH

*delicate golden color*

## MATERIALS:

2 cups flour

1 cup salt

¼ cup instant coffee

¾ to 1 cup warm water

varnish

cup

bowl

bread board

plastic wrap

foil-lined

cookie sheet

## PROCESS:

1. mix flour and salt together in bowl
2. make a well in the center
3. add coffee to water in cup and stir
4. pour coffee-water into flour-salt well, stirring
5. form a ball
   *note:* add more flour or water if necessary
6. knead until smooth on lightly floured board, about 5 minutes
7. wrap in plastic and refrigerate until ready to use
8. model as with any clay
9. bake 325° for 1½ hours, until hard, on foil-lined cookie sheet
10. varnish cooled project to seal

## HINTS:

1. dough is delicate golden color
2. work on foil-lined cookie sheets
3. roll dough ½'' thick for success
4. enough dough for one 8-inch flat project or several small projects

# CINNAMON DOUGH

*smells nice, but inedible*

## MATERIALS:

2 cups flour
1 cup salt
5 t. cinnamon

¾ to 1 cup warm water
bowl
cookie sheets

bread board
plastic wrap

## PROCESS:

1. mix flour, salt, and cinnamon in bowl
2. make a well in center
3. pour in water
4. mix with hands until dough forms a ball
   *hint:* more flour or water may be added so dough is neither crumbly nor sticky
5. knead on lightly floured board until smooth and satiny, about 5 minutes
6. wrap in plastic and refrigerate 20 minutes before using
7. use as any clay
   *note:* excellent for cookie cutter ornaments rolled ¾" thick
8. bake 350° 1 hour, until hard

## VARIATIONS:

1. sandpaper and varnish when cool
2. when working, pieces may be added by dipping them in water or brushing piece with water and pressing on work
3. work on a cookie sheet for easy clean-up
4. other ideas —
   use garlic press for hair
   thread ribbon through to hang
   trace patterns and cut
   make candy cane shapes, peppermint balls, or chocolate kisses
   use dough candies to decorate wreaths

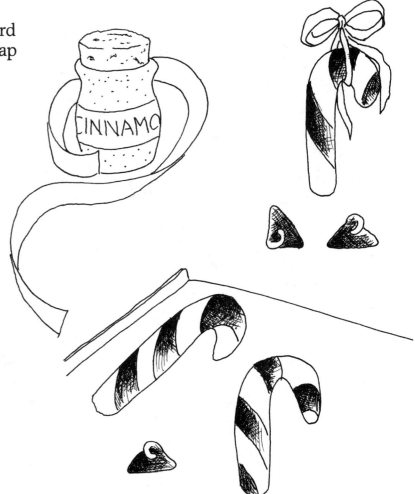

# SOAPY DOUGH

*soap gives dough a nice fragrance*

**MATERIALS:**
2 cups flour
½ cup salt
2 T. liquid tempera paint
1 T. liquid soap
water
bowl

**PROCESS:**
1. mix all ingredients except water in bowl
2. add water to make a workable dough
3. model as with any dough

# CORNMEAL DOUGH

*forms smooth dough — keeps well*

**MATERIALS:**
1½ cups flour
1½ cups cornmeal
1 cup salt
1 cup water
bowl

**PROCESS:**
1. mix all ingredients in bowl
2. add more water to form smooth dough
3. model as with any dough
   *hint:* keeps up to six weeks in airtight container

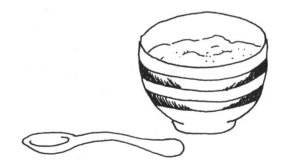

# OATMEAL DOUGH

*a sticky but unique dough — inedible*

## MATERIALS:

| | | |
|---|---|---|
| 1 cup flour | or . . . | 1 part flour |
| 2 cups oatmeal | | 2 parts oatmeal |
| 1 cup water | bowl | 1 part water |

## PROCESS:

1. gradually add water to flour and oatmeal in bowl
2. knead until mixed
   *hint:* this dough is sticky, but unique in texture
3. model as with any clay

## VARIATIONS:

1. add cornmeal in small quantity for texture
2. add coffee grounds in small quantity for texture

# COTTON DOUGH

*cotton puffs up and holds shape*

**MATERIALS:**
1 cup flour
¾ to 1 cup water
1 bag small cotton balls
bowl
cookie sheet

**PROCESS:**
1. mix flour and water in bowl until smooth paste
2. coat cotton balls in paste
   *hint:* they tend to puff up and stay if handled gently
3. allow excess mixture to fall off each ball
4. form balls into desired shapes
5. place on cookie sheet
6. bake 325° for 1 hour, until lightly browned and hard

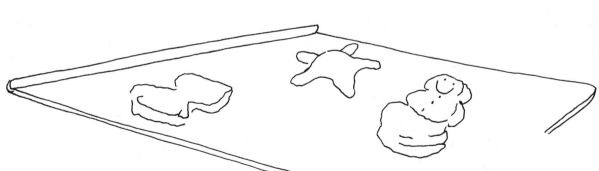

# GLUE DOUGH

*common ingredients — nice, white dough*

**MATERIALS:**
1 cup flour
1 cup cornstarch
½ cup white glue
water
bowl

**PROCESS:**
1. mix flour, cornstarch, and glue in bowl
2. add water as needed
3. knead until workable
4. model and explore dough freely

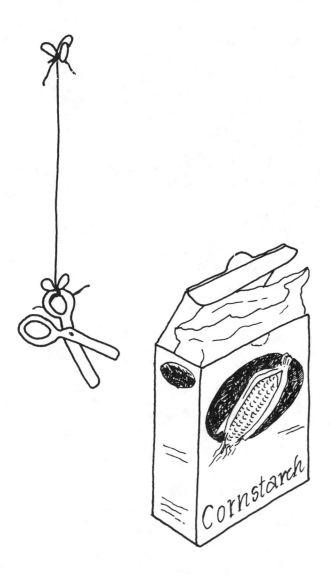

# SHAMPOO DOUGH

**MATERIALS:**
¾ cup flour
¼ cup white glue
¼ cup thick shampoo
bowl
paint, optional

**PROCESS:**
1. mix all ingredients in bowl
2. knead
3. add more flour if needed
4. model, or roll out and cut
5. dry
6. paint if desired

# VINEGAR DOUGH

*good basic playdough*

**MATERIALS:**
3 cups flour
1 cup salt
1 cup water
¼ cup oil
2 T. vinegar
bowl

**PROCESS:**
1. mix all ingredients in bowl
2. add more water if necessary
3. knead
4. model as with any dough

**HINTS:**
1. keeps well in plastic bag
2. knead water into dough to refresh

# BEAD CLAY

*beads make lovely gifts*

**MATERIALS:**

¾ cup flour
½ cup salt
½ cup cornstarch
warm water
bowl

toothpicks
string
paint
sealant (optional)

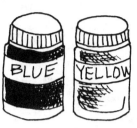 

**PROCESS:**

1. mix flour, salt, and cornstarch in bowl
2. add warm water gradually until mixture forms a shape
3. knead
4. make beads, pierce with toothpicks, and allow to dry
5. paint and string
6. seal, if desired

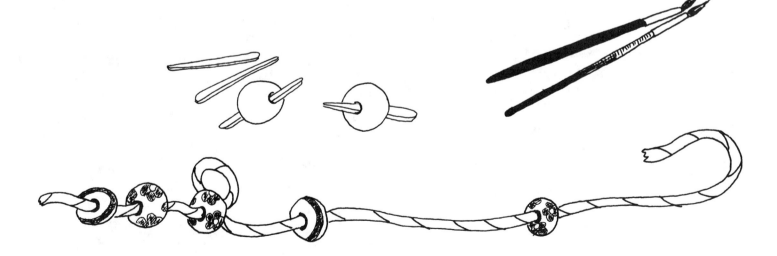

# MAP MODELING 1

*excellent for dioramas and maps —*
*dries in 1-2 days*

## MATERIALS:

| | |
|---|---|
| 1 part salt | food coloring or paints |
| 1 part flour | heavy cardboard |
| ⅔ part water | bowl |

## PROCESS:

1. mix salt and flour in bowl
2. add enough water until like thick frosting
3. stir
4. add food coloring before molding, or mold and paint when dry
5. draw map on heavy cardboard
6. spread mixture on cardboard, adding hills and valleys
7. dry
8. paint if desired

## HINTS:

1. excellent for box dioramas
2. use to build free form designs
3. make fantasy maps of imaginary towns, islands, worlds

# MAP MODELING 2

*dries harder than mixture one,
in 1-3 days — keeps indefinitely*

## MATERIALS:
2 parts salt
1 part flour
1 part water
food coloring or tempera paints
heavy cardboard
bowl

## PROCESS:
1. mix salt and flour in bowl
2. add water until like icing
3. stir
4. add food coloring in small amounts and stir until blended
   or, paint dried project
5. use at once
6. spread mixture on heavy cardboard
7. build up mountains a little at a time by drying each layer
8. dry
9. paint if desired

## HINTS:
1. mixture takes 1 to 3 days to dry
2. white grainy texture
3. dries to harder surface than mixture one
4. takes longer to dry than mixture one
5. keeps indefinitely when dry

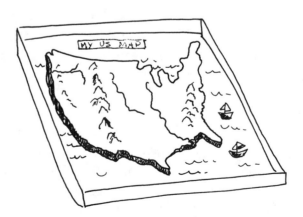

# CREPE PAPER MODELING

*makes unusual sculptures*

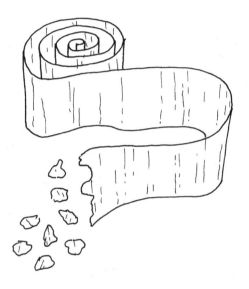

## MATERIALS:
2 cups crepe paper, confetti-sized    water    shellac (optional)
1 T. salt                             plastic
1 cup flour                           bowl

## PROCESS:
1. cover table with plastic or oilcloth
2. tear crepe paper into tiny confetti-sized pieces
3. place in a bowl
4. add enough water to cover crepe paper
5. soak 15 minutes until soft
6. mix flour and salt together
7. add enough flour-salt mixture to crepe paper to make a stiff dough
8. knead the mixture
9. cover a bowl or dish with wax paper or plastic
10. cover this mold with crepe paper clay
    *hint:* make a thick layer, smoothing around the edges of the mold
11. let dry for 2 days to harden
12. remove bowl from mold and paint, if desired
13. shellac will give a high gloss and preserve project

## VARIATIONS:
use crepe paper clay —
1. over a mold such as balls of newspaper
2. over tubes of newspaper forming an animal shape or other sculpture shape
3. over a wire form or other armature

# CREPE PAPER JEWELRY

*perfect for beads*

## MATERIALS:

1 cup crepe paper clippings (one color)
1 cup warm water
½ to ⅔ cup wheat flour
bowl

board
needle, toothpick, or string
sandpaper (optional)

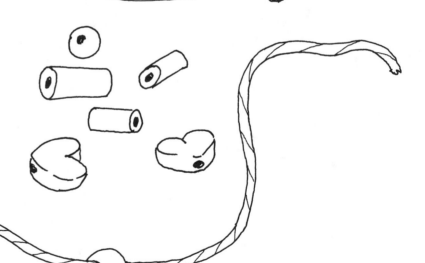

## PROCESS:

1. chop paper very fine
2. place in bowl and cover with water
3. set aside several hours, until soft and pliable
4. pour off excess water
5. add ½ cup flour and stir
6. pour out onto a floured board and knead
7. add enough flour to make a piecrust type dough
8. model clay into beads of any shapes and sizes
9. push a needle through the bead or mold around a toothpick or piece of heavy string
10. dries to a hard finish
11. sand if desired

# SAWDUST MIXTURE

*putty-like dough*

**MATERIALS:**
1 cup sawdust
½ cup Wallpaper Paste (see page 94)
water
bowl
paint (optional)

**PROCESS:**
1. mix sawdust with Wallpaper Paste in bowl
2. add enough water to make mixture like soft putty
3. squeeze and pat modeling mixture to desired shape
4. paint when dry, if desired

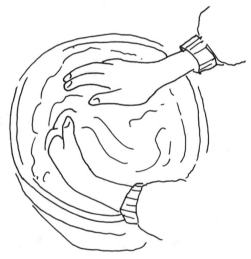

# BREAD DOUGH
## chapter 2

Although many of the following recipes are not made with yeast, all are considered "bread doughs" based upon the resulting finished product. Some are actually made with slices of bread combined with other ingredients. All of the following art experiences are open-ended in the final outcome based upon the child's own creative ideas and exploration.

# WORKING WITH BREAD DOUGHS

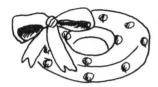

**CREATING THE OBJECT:**
**Basic Process:**

1. all dough parts must be joined with water, using a brush or fingers
2. adhere thin pieces of dough by pushing an instrument through them like the eraser of a pencil, toothpick, screwdriver
3. shape objects directly on a baking sheet or piece of foil on a sheet. Teflon or aluminium.
4. impressing can be done with any variety of objects
5. cut straight edges with a sharp knife, pizza cutters, carrot slicers
6. ragged edges can be smoothed by a finger dipped in water
7. small objects can be baked solid
8. large pieces can be baked over foil shapes
9. very small objects can be baked on toothpicks
10. add hanging devices before baking: ornament hooks, bent wire, circles from pop top drink cans, paper clips
11. hair, fringe, and similar effects are created by pushing dough through a garlic press, or lengths of cooked spaghetti can be added (raw noodles or pasta in any shape can be added to dough and then baked)
12. sequins, plastics, metallic fabrics can be baked into the dough at low temperatures.
13. branches, twigs, pods, acorns, seeds, shells, can be baked into dough
14. breaks and cracks in baked pieces can be repaired with white glue forced into the crack...fresh dough can be added between broken pieces then rebaked and covered with paint
15. if an object softens, rebake and reseal
16. do not eat this dough

**BAKING THIS DOUGH:**

1. bake until thoroughly dried and almost rock hard
2. 275°-325° for ½ hour per ¼ inch thickness (dough remains whiter at lower temperatures)
3. if a part browns more than another part, cover the brown with foil and finish baking

## PRECOLORING AND GLAZING:
Some coloring may be added before and during baking (use whole wheat and rye for precoloring)

### Before Baking:
1. add food paste or food coloring, tube watercolors, colored ink, or fabric dyes
2. paste coloring will be vivid, liquid will be more pastel

### During Baking:
The more applications of glaze during baking, the darker it becomes, using a soft bristle paintbrush
1. egg
   beat egg with a fork, add 1 T. water
   try the yolk mixed with water
   try diluting with acrylic paint and water or food coloring
2. mayonnaise
   same as egg
3. condensed milk
   sometimes yields a marbelized or splotch effect
   add spices such as curry, cinnamon, or turmeric
4. instant coffee
   add 2 T. to egg or milk for a brown glaze
5. water
   brush a thin coat over before baking
6. liquid shoe polish and colored leather dyes
   brush or rub after the first 15 minutes of baking

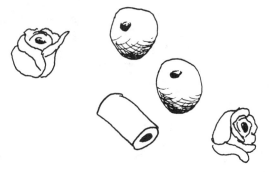

## FINISHING:
1. SURFACE COLORANTS

   | | |
   |---|---|
   | acrylic paints | vegetable coloring |
   | watercolor | colored pencils |
   | felt tip pens | tempera or poster paint |
   | pen and ink | varnish stains |
   | fabric dyes | gesso |
   | cosmetics | |

   acrylics are the most popular and efficient coloring
2. PAINT BRUSHES
   always clean brushes after using and dry

## SEALING:
Sealing prevents moisture from causing mold
   varnish
   lacquer
   clear white glue
   spray painting

# BASIC BREADCRAFT

*versatile, easy, basic
inedible*

## MATERIALS:

| | | |
|---|---|---|
| 4 cups flour | bowl | plastic |
| 1½ cups warm water | baking sheet | foil |
| 1 cup salt | board | wax paper |

## PROCESS:

1. combine flour and salt in bowl
2. make well in center
3. pour in 1 cup water, mixing with hands
4. add more water and continue mixing
   *note:* not crumbly or sticky, but should form a ball
5. knead 5 minutes on floured board, until smooth
6. work with small portion of dough at a time
7. wrap remainder in plastic and put in refrigerator
   *hint:* if dough dries out, add a few drops of water and knead
8. work on foil or wax paper
9. bake 1 hour or until hard at 325°
   *hint:* dough should not "give" when tapped with knife

## VARIATIONS:

use for —

| | |
|---|---|
| napkin rings | jewelry |
| wall plaques | beads |
| pretend rolls, pretzels, bagels | molds and impressions |
| as cranberries to string | bugs, insects, animals |
|   with popcorn | free form objects |
| pretend fruits, vegetables, and meats | |
| picture frames | |

# COLORED DOUGH

**MATERIALS:**
Basic Breadcraft dough (page 56)

**PROCESS:**
1. squeeze small amount of acrylic paint or food coloring into a ball of dough
2. knead
3. model as with Basic Breadcraft dough
   *hint:* colored dough will look lighter when dried or baked

**VARIATIONS:**
1. use for —
   valentines                    shamrocks
   creatures                     holiday symbols
   pumpkins                      cookie shapes and more
2. make several batches in different colors

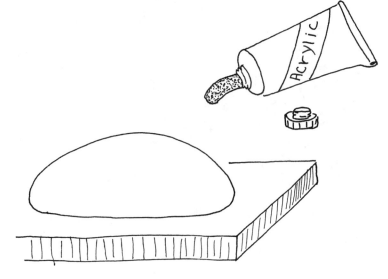

# PATTI'S BREAD CLAY

*half the basic recipe —*
*different baking technique*

## MATERIALS:
⅔ cup warm water        wooden spoon
½ cup salt              bowl
2 cups flour

## PROCESS:
1. mix water and salt with wooden spoon in bowl
2. add flour and stir
3. knead
4. model and explore dough
5. bake at 225° or 250° for 4 to 6 hours
   *hint:* should be hard on both sides

## VARIATIONS:
1. mix in liquid tempera for color at step one
2. paint and seal

# BRICK BREAD

*bakes to a rock-hard finish —*
*inedible*

## MATERIALS:

| | | |
|---|---|---|
| 1 pkg. yeast | 2 t. salt | bowl |
| ¼ cup warm water | 5 to 8 cups flour | dish |
| 1½ cups scalded milk | 2 eggs and brush | pan |
| 1 T. shortening | ¼ to ⅓ cup plaster of paris | fork |
| 2 T. sugar | towel | foil-lined cookie sheet |
| | | varnish |

## PROCESS:

1. mix yeast in warm water in dish
2. scald milk over medium heat in pan and add shortening
3. cool
4. add sugar to yeast
5. mix milk mixture, yeast mixture, flour, salt, and plaster of paris
6. place in greased bowl in oven to warm, turned off
7. cover with towel and let rise for about 1 hour, until double
8. punch air out of dough and let rest 10 minutes
9. model as with any clay, or shape into loaves, rolls, bagels or pretzels
   *uses:* makes pretend breads, sculptures, picture frames, wall hanging, etc.

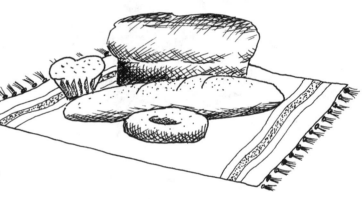

10. let rise another ½ to 1 hour until doubled
11. bake on foil-lined sheet at 350° for 15 minutes
12. brush with beaten eggs
13. bake another 15 minutes
14. reduce oven to 150°, and bake 6 hours
    *hint:* dough should sound hollow when tapped with knife
15. turn all pieces and bake two more hours
16. cool
17. begin coating with varnish at least 4 times in all
    *hint:* to add poppy seeds, sesame seeds, or sprinkles, put on when second coat is sticky

# FROZEN BREAD DOUGH

*the easiest of edible bread doughs*

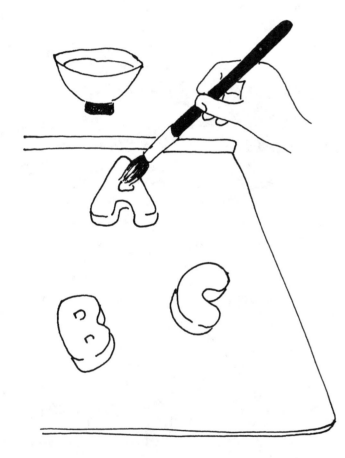

## MATERIALS:
loaf of frozen bread dough  
  (from freezer section of  
  grocery store)  
1 egg  
salt or sugar and cinnamon  

greased cookie sheet  
small bowl  
brush  
pan and water  

## PROCESS:
1. thaw frozen bread dough night before using
2. shape into small balls
3. preheat oven and grease cookie sheet
4. separate out egg white and discard yolk  
   *hint:* yolk can be saved for glazing projects
5. beat white with 1 or 2 t. water in bowl
6. place pan of boiling water in oven to help texture of bread
7. let rise
8. use dough like any clay
9. place dough shapes on cookie sheet
10. brush egg white on dough shapes, and sprinkle salt or sugar-cinnamon over shapes
11. bake for 20 minutes at 350°

## VARIATIONS:
| | | | |
|---|---|---|---|
| letters | snakes | shapes | numbers |
| pretzels | animals, lying down | decorations | and more |

# BROWN BREAD MODELING

*nice option to white flour —
makes 2 cups brown dough*

**MATERIALS:**
½ cup plain salt
¾ cup hot water
2 cups whole-wheat flour
1 T. vegetable oil
bowl
cookie sheet
foil

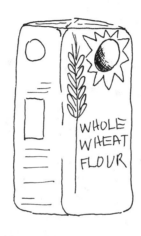

**PROCESS:**
1. dissolve salt in water in a bowl
2. add flour and oil
3. mix with hands and knead
   *hint:* keep hands wet
4. mold, or roll out and cut
5. bake on foil-lined cookie sheet at 300° for 1 hour

**VARIATIONS:**
excellent for —
1. plaques
2. holiday decorations
3. jewelry

**HINT:**
makes about 2 cups

# ROSE PETAL BEADS

*pretty and unique — enough for one necklace*

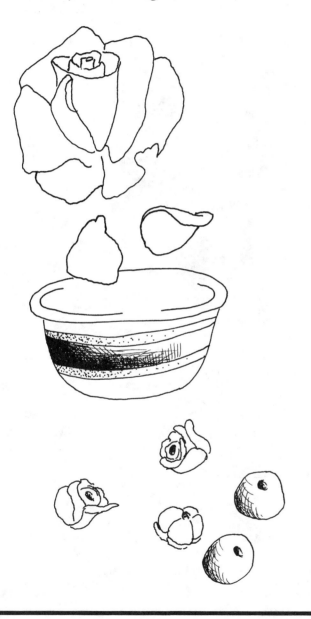

## MATERIALS:
½ cup flour
1 T. salt
2 T. water
3 cups rose petals
round toothpicks
bowl

## PROCESS:
1. mix flour, salt, and water to stiff dough in bowl
2. cut rose petals into tiny pieces and crush in palms
3. mix crushed petals into dough without making it crumbly
4. shape dough into beads
5. push toothpicks through center to make holes
6. dry for a few days
7. string beads on cord after thoroughly dry

## HINTS:
1. makes enough beads for 1 necklace
2. remove toothpicks before dough gets too hard

## VARIATIONS:
1. scratch rose designs into wet beads
2. make different shaped beads
3. experiment with other sculptures

# CORNSTARCH BREAD

*good use for day-old bread —*
*dries without cracking*

**MATERIALS:**
10 slices white bread
½ t. cornstarch
4 T. white glue
2-3 T. water
bowl

**PROCESS:**
1. tear crust off bread for birds
2. shread white bread into fine crumbs in bowl
3. add cornstarch and mix
4. add glue and water, mixing with hands into a ball
   *hint:* add more water if necessary
5. knead until smooth and elastic — 10 minutes
6. model objects
   *hint:* this dough cuts and rolls out thin and smooth
          and dries without cracking
7. finish with acrylic paints

**VARIATIONS:**
to color —
1. separate dough into several balls
2. squeeze liquid or paste type food coloring into dough
3. knead
4. if too dark, add more plain dough
   *hint:* colors in this dough do not dry lighter or darker

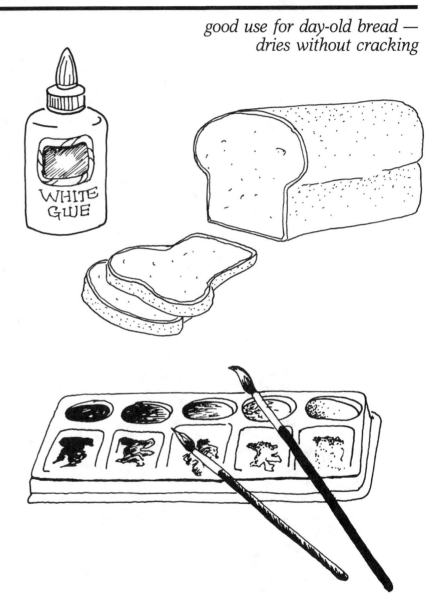

# BREAD AND GLUE DOUGH

*children love to make this*

## MATERIALS:
3 slices white bread (any kind)
3 T. white glue
*optional:* 1 t. white shoe polish or acrylic paint
        1 t. glycerin from drugstore
        ½ t. liquid detergent
        3 drops lemon juice
* use *at least* one of the optional ingredients, *or* all of them
bowl
plastic bag
optional glaze

## PROCESS:
1. remove crusts and tear bread into small pieces in bowl
2. mix ingredients together until it no longer sticks to fingers and is smooth (6-10 minutes)
   *hint:* rub a few drops of glycerin on hands to prevent sticking
3. after kneading, place in plastic bag
4. model as with any clay
5. dry 24 hours
6. glaze if desired

# EASY BREAD CLAY

**MATERIALS:**
1 slice white bread
1 T. white glue
¼ t. water
food coloring
clear glaze or clear nail polish

**PROCESS:**
1. cut or tear crust from bread and discard
2. pour glue, then water, onto the slice of bread
3. knead until dough doesn't stick to fingers (10 minutes)
4. divide into parts and add food coloring to each
5. knead until blended
6. work with only a small portion of clay at a time
7. shape objects
8. dry overnight
9. when dry, spray with clear glaze or paint with clear nail polish

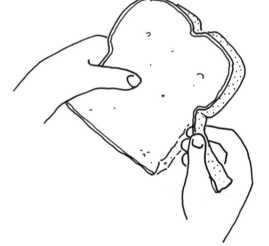

**HINTS:**
1. stores in refrigerator for several days
2. store in plastic bag, storing colors separately

# BREAD MODELING

*has a smooth, satiny finish —*
*enough for 2 or 3 small objects*

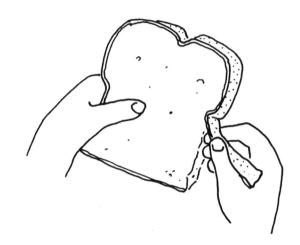

## MATERIALS:
2 slices day old white bread
2 T. white glue
2 drops glycerine
4 drops white vinegar
food coloring or poster paint
bowl

## PROCESS:
1. cut or tear crust from bread and discard
2. break bread into small pieces in a bowl
3. add glue, glycerine, vinegar
4. mix and knead with hands until smooth and pliable
5. divide dough and add coloring
6. knead until color is blended
7. dry 1 to 2 days

## HINTS:
1. makes enough for two or three small objects
2. use lotion on hands to prevent sticking to hands
3. excellent for jewelry, flowers and doll body parts
4. project will have smooth, satiny finish
5. store in plastic bag in refrigerator several days

## VARIATIONS:
"Porcelain Finish"
1. paint pieces with 2 or 3 coats of white glue and thinned
   with water
2. allow each coat to dry before adding the next
3. bake at 225° for 4 minutes

# PLASTER OF PARIS
chapter 3

Plaster of paris is a medium with exciting results for children. The permanence and hardness of the finished art project is often a new and exciting experience. The following 17 art experiences are so easy and fun that there is no need to shy away from this medium. Through experimenting and exploring plaster of paris, children will come to appreciate its unique qualities.

### PLASTER OF PARIS CLEANUP

Begin to clean up immediately after pouring the plaster in the mold. It will harden rapidly once the chemical reaction takes place. Any excess plaster remaining should be wiped from the pan immediately and rolled in newspaper so that it might be disposed of more easily. Do not wash plaster down the drain!! It can harden in the pipes. When cleaning any hands, tools, and mixing pan, be sure the water runs continuously.

*hint:* Mix plaster in a rubber school playground ball cut in half. Easy clean-up. Ball can be turned inside out and the plaster will crack and fall out easily into the trash.

# SAND CAST

*easiest of sand casting ideas*

**MATERIALS:**
box
foil
sand
spoon
coffee can
plaster of paris
paper clip

**PROCESS:**
1. line box with foil
2. scoop sand into box and sprinkle water
3. stick finger into sand to make holes
4. use other ideas to make designs or holes
5. pour plaster (loose whipped cream) over design
6. smooth top of plaster with spoon
7. stick paper clip into plaster as a hook
   *hint:* casting will dry very slowly because of the wet sand
8. after several days, remove casting and hang

# MOSAIC SAND CAST

**MATERIALS:**
plaster of paris
water
clean wet sand
container and spoon to mix plaster
possibly buckets, basins, or pans for sand and water
shells, beach pebbles, driftwood

**PROCESS:**
1. make a clean impression in any wet sand
   *hint:* use a shell, piece of driftwood, handprint, footprint, or a free form
2. inlay impression with decorative items such as shells, beachglass, pebbles, or other collage items
3. mix plaster according to box
   *hint:* prepare small batches as it hardens quickly
4. pour wet plaster into impression
   *hint:* insert paper clip if hanging project is desired
5. harden for 15 to 20 minutes
6. remove plaster form from the impression and brush loose sand from surface
   *hint:* some sand will cling and is part of the art

**VARIATIONS:**
1. do this activity indoors in a box of sand
2. do sand casting in a sandtable
3. work outside in a sand pile or at the beach

# MOSAIC IN PLASTER

*just like a real artist*

## MATERIALS:

bottom of small gift box
sheet of foil
cord
coffee can
plaster of paris

long stirring stick
food coloring
plastic spoon
small smooth stones
scissors

## PROCESS:

1. line bottom of box with foil, pressing into corners
2. to hang later, punch two holes on underside of box and insert cord
3. fill coffee can half full with plaster of paris
4. stirring, add water until mixture looks like heavy cream (add a bit of food coloring now if you wish)
5. pour plaster into foil-lined box
6. quickly spread and smooth the plaster
7. push pebbles halfway into the plaster
8. plaster will dry quickly — about ½ hour
9. display in box

## VARIATIONS:

1. to remove mosaic from box, trim away foil with scissors
2. use other objects such as buttons, seeds, beans, or old jewelry broken apart for mosaic design

# LEAF CASTING

*delicate art experience*

**MATERIALS:**
pie tin
tin can
tree leaves
plaster of paris
spoon
paper clip
optional tempera or watercolor paints

**PROCESS:**
1. fill pie tin with water
2. pour water into the can
3. fill pie tin *again* half full, and add to can
4. wet smooth side of leaf and stick to bottom of tin
5. stirring, add enough plaster to water to make "whipped cream"
6. spoon onto leaf and spread until covered
7. fill rest of pie tin with plaster
8. set paper clip into plaster near edge as a hook
9. the plaster is dry when it is cool
10. remove from pie tin carefully
11. remove leaf

**VARIATIONS:**
1. paint plaster before removing leaf
2. remove leaf and paint leaf's indentation only

# ICE CUBE SCULPTURE

*always surprising results*

## MATERIALS:
plaster of paris
container for mixing plaster
waxed carton
mixing bowl
dull knife
ice cubes
sandpaper

## PROCESS:
1. mix plaster in container
2. fill wax carton with ice, ¾ full
3. fill wax carton with plaster
4. allow to set
5. carefully cut off carton over waste basket or bucket
6. let ice melt
7. cut semi-dry block with dull knife, if desired
8. let dry and finish with sandpaper

## VARIATIONS:
1. paint with tempera
2. paint with oils
3. paint with water colors
4. rub with shoe polish in any color

# BALLOON CREATURES

**MATERIALS:**
balloons
plaster of paris
can
spoon
funnel, large opening
paint, decorations (optional)

**PROCESS:**
1. stirring, mix plaster until creamy
2. pour into an empty balloon using funnel
3. set plaster filled balloon on table and hold until firm
4. then let go and allow to dry at least ½ hour
5. tear off balloon
6. decorate and paint as animals, creatures, or wonderful designs of unknown origin

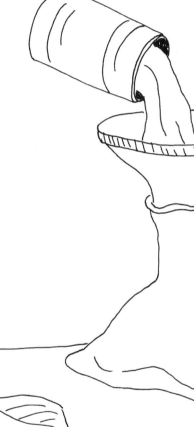

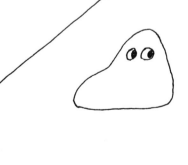

# BAG SCULPTURE

*easy and enjoyable*

## MATERIALS:
plaster of paris
small plastic bag, ziploc preferred
dry tempera, or liquid tempera and brushes

## PROCESS:
1. pour plaster of paris powder into a ziploc bag
2. mix in dry tempera if desired
3. add enough water to form soft dough in bag
4. close the bag
5. squeeze bag with hands to mix water and plaster
6. when warm to the touch, plaster begins to set
7. hold bag in desired shape until plaster hardens
   *hint:* a matter of minutes

## VARIATIONS:
1. paint dry, hard plaster with liquid tempera
2. paint dry, hard plaster with a variety of nail polishes

# FANTASY SCULPTURES

*good for all ages — filled with imagination*

**MATERIALS:**
plastic spoon
plaster of paris
coffee can
sand
wax paper
paint, brushes, optional decorations
spoon

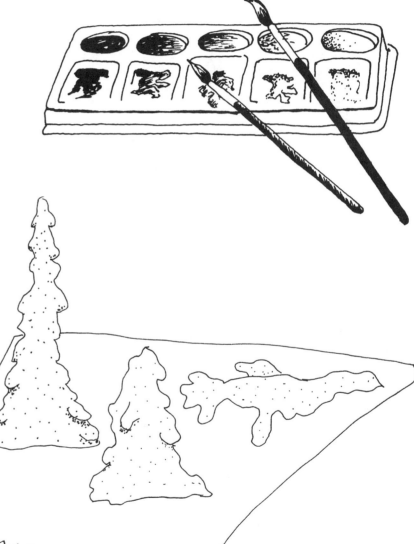

**PROCESS:**
1. stirring, mix water and plaster in coffee can until like thick cream
2. quickly stir enough sand into the plaster of paris to make mixture look like whipped cream, thick
3. pour some of the mixture onto waxed paper creating towering squiggles
4. spoon remaining plaster into long creations
5. squeeze the tall squiggles to create unusual designs (quickly before plaster hardens)
6. when dry, paint and decorate with tempera, sequins, jewels, or beans and seeds

# PUTTY CAST

*highly creative — good group experience*

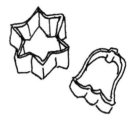

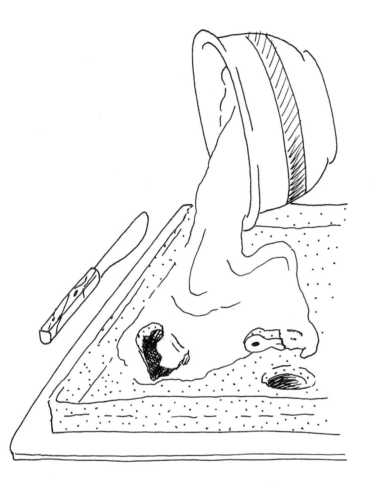

## MATERIALS:
can of putty from hardware store
plaster of paris
plastic wrap
cardboard
knife
rolling pin or cylinder block
objects to make impressions —
   kitchen utensils, toys, cookie cutters, tools

## PROCESS:
1. spread putty on a sheet of plastic wrap on a piece of cardboard
2. roll putty out flat to 1″ thick
3. square off edges of putty, if desired
4. press objects into putty to make designs
5. build a retaining wall of putty around edge of putty base to contain plaster
6. mix plaster and pour into the putty mold to height of retaining wall
7. allow plaster to dry
8. remove by peeling off putty
   *hint:* putty may be reused

## VARIATIONS:
1. coat plaster with wood stain to make designs more visible
2. paint as desired
3. carry putty rectangle outdoors to find ideas for impressions

# SPACKLE RELIEF PANEL

*unique group effort*

## MATERIALS:
very heavy cardboard or plywood for background
box of spackle from hardware store
newspaper, glue, paint, brush
objects for relief: bottle tops, string, scraps, plastic pieces,
  hardware, screws, nails, hooks
sealant (optional)

## PROCESS:
1. arrange collection of objects on background
2. glue everything firmly to the plywood panel or cardboard
   with fast drying glue
3. place on a thick pad of newspaper
4. mix a small amount of spackle according to package
5. scoop up some spackle and coat the entire panel
6. dab on spackle so it covers every object well, but do not
   drown objects
   *hint:* effect is frosted (if not buried under too heavy a coat)
7. dry for several hours or overnight
8. paint panel (optional)
9. varnish or seal with clear acrylic if desired

## VARIATIONS:
**Antique Effect —**
1. spray with metallic paint (gold, silver, copper)
2. dry
3. cover with varnish in a darker tone
4. wipe off wet varnish immediately here and there
5. remove just enough to highlight parts of panel

**Theme Effect —**
gather items that reflect a theme such as:
1. happiness
2. dinosaurs
3. summer
4. multi-cultural

# MARBLE PLASTER

*a nice change - fun to mix*

## MATERIALS:
2 t. white glue
½ cup water
plaster of paris
tempera paint
mold for plaster casting
bowl, soup bowl

## PROCESS:
1. mix glue and water in a bowl
2. stir in enough plaster to make frosting-like mixture
3. pour into soup bowl
4. pour thick coat of tempera paint over mixture
5. fold in color to produce streaks
6. pour into any mold (small milk carton, dixie-cup, etc.)
7. dry

## VARIATIONS:
1. see Sand Casting
2. use any form made of plastic or rubber as a mold

## HINTS:
1. makes about 1 cup — double or triple recipe if desired
2. stronger variation than regular plaster of paris

# SIMULATED MARBLE

*carving is a new experience for most children*

**MATERIALS:**
1 part vermiculite (from plant department)
1 part plaster of paris
water
container for mixing
cardboard box or small milk carton
modeling tools
sandpaper

**PROCESS:**
**1.** mix vermiculite and plaster in mixing container
**2.** add water, stirring constantly until creamy
**3.** pour in box and harden
**4.** carve and model with knife, rasp, sandpaper, nail, or any tool

# ZONALITE SCULPTURE

*unique carving compound*

**MATERIALS:**
zonalite (from local lumberyard)
sand
plaster
pan for mixing
cardboard box
carving tool

**PROCESS:**
1. mix one part of fine sand, one part of zonalite, and two parts of plaster in a mixing container
2. add mixture to water by sifting it through fingers or shaking it from a can or small cup
3. add until sifted mixture builds above the surface of the water
4. stir mixture thoroughly with hands until smooth and creamy, breaking up plaster lumps
5. do not add more water to thin or more plaster to thicken
6. pour into a cardboard container or box lid
7. harden 48 hours
   *hint:* ignore dampness
8. carve the block to desired form using any tools you like

# ALABASTER PLASTER

*lovely — most successful for older children*

## MATERIALS:

2 parts plaster of paris
1 part water
mold suitable for casting
pure white wax or paraffin

bowl
tin can
fine thread or wire
pan of hot water

damp cloth

## PROCESS:

1. mix plaster of paris and water in a bowl
2. stir until creamy
3. pour into a mold, such as the sheets of plastic bubbles that are used to package hardware items, or a shallow dish
4. harden
5. melt wax in tin can set in a pan of hot water over low heat
   THIS STEP IS VERY DANGEROUS FOR CHILDREN
6. remove object from mold
7. tie thread around object and warm in 100° oven
8. dip object by string into melted wax
9. continue dipping until plaster of paris absorbs as much wax as possible
10. hang to dry
11. polish object with a damp cloth after removing string

## HINTS FOR MOLDS:

1. use with any plastic or rubber molds for casting (plastic ice cube trays)
2. save molds that candy comes in at Christmas and Valentine's Day

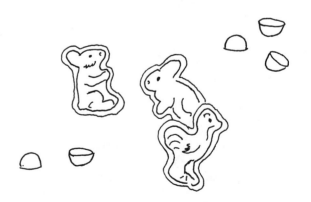

# GESSO PAINTING

*good addition to Gesso Modeling —*
*wide decorative possibilities*

## MATERIALS:
1 t. white glue
1 T. dextrin solution
  (1 cup powdered dextrin
   dissolved in 1 T. hot water)
patching plaster or powdered chalk
cake decorator or brush

small knife
acrylic paints
items to decorate,
  such as a box
bowl

## PROCESS:
1. mix glue with dextrin solution in bowl
2. add patching plaster to make thick paste that will hold shape, but soft enough to apply with brush
3. draw pattern or design on box, picture frames, furniture, etc.
4. fill in design with gesso paint until desired height
5. use brush or cake decorator
6. dry
7. paint with acrylic paints

## HINTS:
1. gesso paint can be carved with a small sharp knife
2. form letters of the alphabet or other designs on wax paper, harden, and then glue to another surface
3. dextrin may be ordered from science and chemistry teachers or through your pharmacy (it is a fine powdered sugar-starch)
4. substitute commercial Gesso from art store

# GESSO MODELING

*unusual ingredients, excellent dough*

## MATERIALS:
1 t. Sobo glue or other white glue
1 T. dextrin solution
   (1 cup powdered dextrin dissolved in 1 T. hot water)
¼ cup plaster of paris, patching plaster, whiting, Bon Ami,
   unscented talcum or powdered chalk
palette knife or putty knife
model enamel, or tempera and shellac
old plate

## PROCESS:
1. pour glue onto plate
2. add dextrin solution and mix
3. add plaster of paris 1 T. at a time
   *hint:* mix with palette knife or putty knife until plaster will
         not absorb any more solution
4. scrape dough together and knead
   *hint:* use plaster like flour to prevent sticking to hands
5. knead several minutes until claylike and pliable
   *hint:* should be stiff enough to hold shape
6. model small objects such as flowers and
   ornaments for attaching to picture frames, boxes,
   plaques
   *hint:* fasten pieces together or to a base with a
         few drops of dextrin solution and a few
         drops of glue and a little plaster
7. dry at least one week before painting
8. apply coat of shellac over tempera

## HINTS:
1. makes enough dough for 2 or 3 small objects
2. mix two batches for larger projects
3. dough made with any materials (except plaster)
   can be stored indefinitely, but must be kept moist
   with a damp cloth in an airtight container
4. dextrin may be ordered from science or
   chemistry teachers or through your pharmacy (it
   is a fine powdered sugar-starch)
5. substitute commercial Gesso from art store

# CLOTH DIPPING

*messy and fun*

## MATERIALS:
1½ parts plaster of paris
1 T. alum for each cup water
1 part water
cloth, gauze, paper towels, or old sheet

## PROCESS:
1. mix plaster of paris and alum
2. add plaster and alum to water
3. stir until smooth and creamy
4. dip cloth into plaster
5. drape over a bottle or armature of any kind
   *hint for armature:* cardboard cone, wire, milk carton,
   paper tubes
6. drape and shape in 15 to 20 minutes before it dries

## HINT:
dries very hard

## VARIATIONS:
1. use to make ghosts or angels
2. use to make strange and interesting shapes
3. can be painted, glittered, or glued with broken jewelry
   when dry

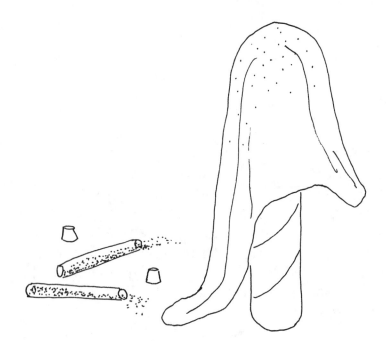

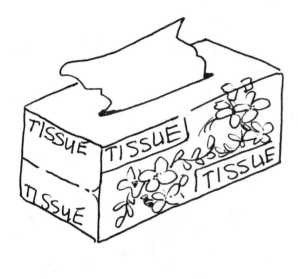

# PAPIER-MACHE
### chapter 4

There is more to papier-mache than meets the eye. Not only does papier-mache work wonders in the traditional way, it can also be a wonderful clay or dough. Enjoy and explore the following 11 art experiences and the many possibilities for each. Feel free to mix and experiment with ideas from one page to another.

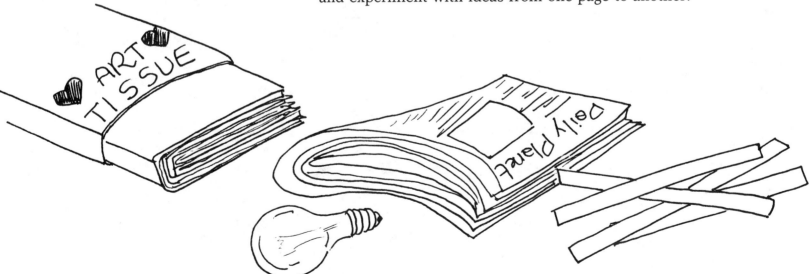

# SOFT PAPIER-MACHE PULP

*must be used immediately*

**MATERIALS:**
paper napkins, tissues, or toilet paper
Thin Paste (see page 96) or white glue

**PROCESS:**
1. crumble napkins or tissue
2. cover with Thin Paste or white glue
3. model to desired shape

**HINT:**
will not store — must be used immediately

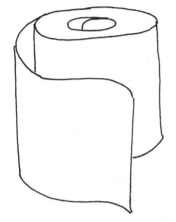

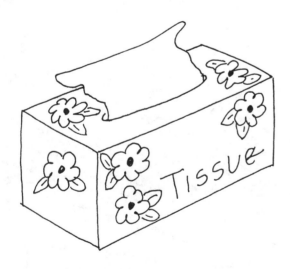

# STRIP PAPIER-MACHE

## MATERIALS:
old newspapers
Wallpaper Paste or Thin Paste (see pages 94 & 96)
balloon, jar, or lightbulb

## PROCESS:
1. tear newspaper into long thin strips from the fold down
2. lay paper strips on a pad of newspaper and cover one side of strips with paste
   or...pull *through* paste, squeezing off extra paste with fingers
3. cover a base such as a balloon, jar, or light bulb with paste covered newspaper strips
   *hint:* lay strips in one direction
4. apply second layer of strips, running these across first layer
5. continue for 4 or 5 layers
6. allow 1 to 2 days to dry

## VARIATIONS:
1. build a shape of newspaper tubes and form strips over this base
2. use to build puppets, piñatas, animals, or other articles

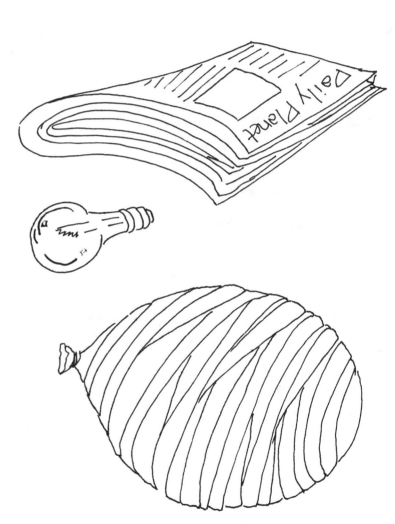

# PAPIER-MACHE PULP

*some say this is easier to use than*
*Strip Papier-Mache — model like clay*

## MATERIALS:
newspaper
1 pail or large pan filled with warm water
electric mixer
Wallpaper Paste (see page 94)
oil of cloves
poster paints, shellac

## PROCESS:
1. tear newspaper into 1 inch strips
2. fill a pail with warm water
3. sprinkle strips into water, stirring to separate
   *hint:* if necessary, add more water until paper is covered
4. set aside overnight
5. beat soaked paper with mixer until smooth
6. strain out excess water by squeezing with hands
7. add paste gradually until clay-like with hands
8. add oil of cloves to prevent mold while drying
9. shape or model as with clay
10. allow to dry 3 to 5 days on a rack
    *hint:* air should circulate around object until completely dry
11. paint with tempera paints and then shellac

## VARIATIONS:
1. mix sawdust or sand into pulp for different textures
2. try using wood stain or shoe polish instead of paint

# PAPIER-MACHE MASH

*models like clay —*
*dries hard and durable*

## MATERIALS:

newspapers
½ gallon water
1 large cooking pot
slotted spoon
quart bowl
electric mixer
collander or wire strainer

1 cup wheat flour
4 drops cinnamon oil
poster or tempera paint
sandpaper
shellac or varnish

## PROCESS:

1. fill bowl with newspaper pieces ½''x 1½''
2. boil water in large pot
3. add newspaper pieces to pot stirring constantly with slotted spoon
4. cook over medium heat 20 minutes until broken down
5. stir occasionally
6. beat with electric mixer until smooth
7. strain through collander, but do not squeeze
8. return paper to pot
9. add flour, mix well, and return to heat on low
10. cook until stiff enough to stand in piles
11. mix in oil of cinnamon
12. pour onto thick newspaper to cool
13. model as with clay
14. allow several days to dry or, bake at 200° until dry
15. when dry, sand until smooth, and paint
16. then shellac or varnish

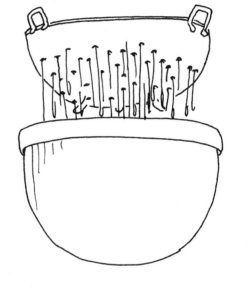

## HINTS:

1. makes enough mash for 1 project (quadruple to make larger objects)
2. dries to hard, durable finish

## VARIATIONS:

1. cover jars, bottles, blocks of wood
2. cover boxes to make furniture, ½'' thick

# TISSUE MACHE

*colored tissues are a pretty papier-mache*

## MATERIALS:
tissues (optional, colored tissue)
liquid starch
liquid glue
bowl or bucket

## PROCESS:
1. tear tissues into pieces or strips
2. soak in starch until mushy in bowl or bucket
3. add liquid glue until pulp holds a form
4. squeeze out excess starch
5. shape
6. dry
7. paint if desired

## VARIATIONS:
cover a form such as —
1. balls of newspaper
2. a milk carton
3. a balloon

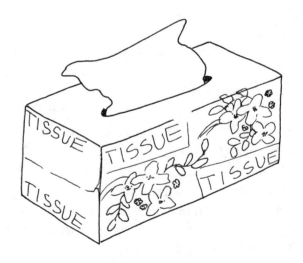

# BOTTLE SCULPTURE

**MATERIALS:**
plastic bottle
Wallpaper Paste (see page 94), water
scissors, newspaper, scrap materials, glue
paint

**PROCESS:**
1. mix Wallpaper Paste with water
2. cut strips of paper, wet, and press onto bottle
3. let dry and then paint

**VARIATIONS:**
1. decorate bottle with scrap materials and glue
2. make large container by cutting plastic gallon jug in half
3. make small container from 6 oz. juice container
4. experiment covering any plastic container
5. rub with shoe polish instead of paint

# FLOUR PAPIER-MACHE

*dough-like quality*

## MATERIALS:

3 parts pulp
1 part flour
⅓ part salt
oil of cloves

old newspapers
water
large pan or bucket
electric mixer
poster or tempera paints
lacquer or shellac

## PROCESS:

1. tear 1"x 1½" pieces into large pan or bucket of water
2. stir until each piece is wet
3. set aside overnight
4. beat newspaper pieces to pulp with mixer
5. squeeze water from pulp until moist, but not dry
6. mix flour and salt together and add to pulp until smooth and claylike
   *hint:* if too moist, add more flour
7. add oil of cloves to prevent mold while drying
8. model like clay or build up over a form
9. allow 3 to 5 days to dry
10. paint with tempera paints
11. cover with lacquer for water proofing (cover with shellac if not waterproofing)

CAUTION

# SAWDUST MODELING

*like clay — woodgrain appearance*

**MATERIALS:**

1 cup fine sawdust       jar
food coloring (optional)
old newspaper
1 cup Thin Paste or Paper Paste (see page 95 & 96)
shellac or clear varnish (optional)

**PROCESS:**

1. mix sawdust with food coloring in a jar
2. drain and spread on newspaper to dry
3. mix sawdust and paste to thick dough
4. knead
    *hint:* if sawdust is coarse, more paste may be needed
5. model as with any clay
    *hint:* stick bits of dough to piece with water
6. dries within 2 to 3 days
    or, bake at 200° for 1 to 2 hours
7. for a permanent finish, spray with shellac or varnish

**HINTS:**

1. makes 1 cup
2. woodgrain appearance
3. can be sanded for smoother finish

# WALLPAPER PASTE

*makes 1½ gallons — use with Papier-Mache Pulp and Bottle Sculptures*

## MATERIALS:
4 cups flour
1 cup sugar
1 gallon warm water
1 quart cold water
½ T. oil of cinnamon (optional)
large pan

## PROCESS:
1. mix flour and sugar in large pan
2. add enough warm water to make smooth paste
3. then add rest of warm water, stirring
4. boil, stirring until thick and clear
5. thin with 1 quart cold water
6. add oil of cinnamon if paste will not be used same day
7. use with Strip Papier-Mache and other projects using large amounts of paste

## HINTS:
1. spreads best when warm
2. keeps for a few days
3. makes 1½ gallons
4. use to cover lamp shades and wastebaskets with cloth or wallpaper

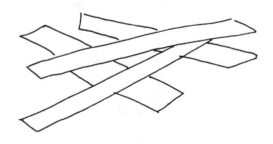

# PAPER PASTE

*makes 1 cup — use with Sawdust Modeling*

**MATERIALS:**

⅓ cup flour spoon
2 T. sugar brush or
1 cup water tongue depressor
¼ t. oil of cinnamon (optional)
saucepan

**PROCESS:**

1. mix flour and sugar in saucepan
2. gradually add water, stirring vigorously
3. cook over low until clear, stirring
4. remove from stove and add oil, stir
5. spread with brush or tongue depressor

**HINTS:**

1. soft, smooth and thick
2. makes 1 cup
3. good spreading consistency
4. stores covered in a jar for several weeks without refrigeration

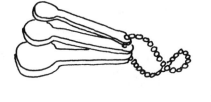

# THIN PASTE

*stores several months —
use with Soft Papier-Mache Pulp*

## MATERIALS:
¼ cup sugar
¼ cup flour
½ t. alum
1¾ cup water
¼ t. oil of cinnamon (optional)
medium pan
brush or tongue depressor

## PROCESS:
1. mix sugar, flour, and alum in pan
2. add 1 cup water gradually, stirring vigorously
3. boil until clear and smooth, stirring
4. add remaining water, and oil of cinnamon
5. stir
6. spread with brush or tongue depressor

## HINTS:
1. makes 1 pint
2. stores for several months without refrigeration

# EDIBLE ART DOUGH
### chapter 5

The 23 art doughs in this chapter could be the favorites for all ages. Not only do they taste good, they also model beautifully and easily. From the exploratory doughs such as Peanut Butter Playdough to the highly sophisticated Gingerbread Architectural Dough, this chapter will be a delight for the creative, exploring child.

*note:* Wash hands before working with food. Be aware of sanitation when working with food in a group, especially when children will be eating food prepared by others.

# SCULPTURE COOKIE DOUGH

*delicious, excellent modeling dough*

## MATERIALS:

5½ cups flour
3 t. baking soda
1¾ cups sugar
¼ t. salt
¼ cup honey
1 t. vanilla
3 t. grated lemon or oranges, optional
1 cup (½ pound) butter or margarine
½ cup boiling water
1 egg, lightly beaten

large bowl, smaller bowl
plastic wrap
spoon or mixer
greased cookie sheets
cooling racks

## PROCESS:

1. in large bowl, combine flour and baking soda
2. in another bowl, combine sugar, salt, honey, vanilla, and lemon peel
3. add butter and water to sugar mixture and beat until sugar is dissolved
4. gradually stir in flour mixture until stiff, using hands
5. use immediately
   *hint:* cover with wrap and refrigerate up to 2 days or freeze, but bring dough to room temperature before shaping
6. use cutters on rolled dough (⅛'' to ¼'' thick) or make free form sculptures by pinching, rolling, or cutting dough
7. place 1 inch apart on cookie sheet
8. brush with beaten egg if desired
9. bake at 300° for 20-30 minutes, or golden at edges
10. cool 10 minutes on sheets, then move to cooling racks to finish cooling

## HINT:
to store, wrap sculptures airtight and store at room
temperature for up to 2 weeks, or freeze

## VARIATIONS:
### Cookie-Cutter Composites
1. roll out and cut dough
2. arrange cutouts on greased sheets
3. combine shapes and overlap edges to build decorative
   images
4. bake and cool

### Appliques on Cutouts
1. roll out directly on a greased baking sheet if large, or on a
   floured board for smaller
2. cut out shapes with cutters, or make paper patterns to
   trace and cut
3. for appliques shape small pieces of dough into dabs, dots,
   tiny ropes, or any free form
4. press appliques onto the cookie base
   *hint:* do not build to thicker than ¾″
5. bake and cool

## GIFT IDEA
wrap in clear or colored cellophane and tape or heat seal

## HEAT SEAL
1. line a baking sheet with paper towels in 325° oven
2. wrap each sculpture firmly in plastic wrap, taping if
   necessary
3. place on warm baking sheet in oven
4. heat for 2 minutes until plastic shrinks tightly over
   sculptures
5. remove and cool

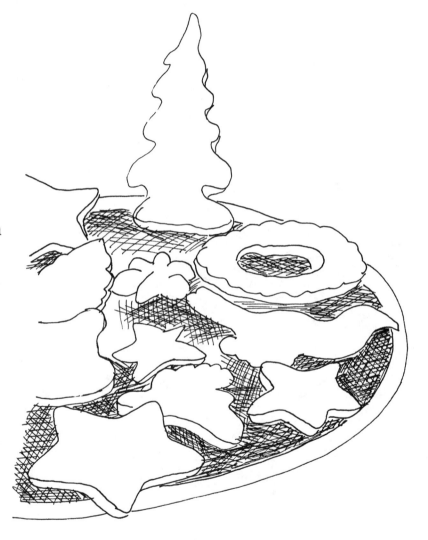

*allow for creative designs*

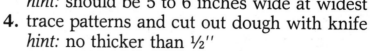

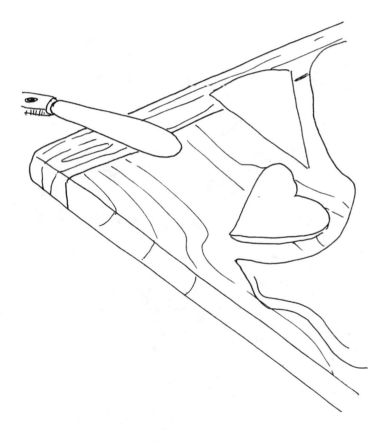

## MATERIALS:
bowl / mixer / cookie sheets
popsicle sticks or craft sticks
assorted candy decoration, optional

**beat —**
⅔ cup solid shortening
⅔ cup butter or margarine, soft
¾ cup sugar
¾ cup brown sugar

**add and beat —**
2 eggs
2 t. vanilla

**in another bowl, mix —**
3½ cups flour
2 t. baking powder
1 t. salt
4 t. pumpkin pie spice,
   or 1 t. each allspice, cinnamon, ginger, and nutmeg

## PROCESS:
1. mix flour mixture with butter mixture
   *hint:* use hands or mixer
2. cover and refrigerate for 1 to 2 hours
3. cut free form cookie patterns from heavy paper or
   old file folders
   *hint:* should be 5 to 6 inches wide at widest point
4. trace patterns and cut out dough with knife
   *hint:* no thicker than ½"

5. transfer cookies with wide spatula to ungreased sheet
   *hint:* space 2 inches apart
6. insert stick 1½″ to 2″ into base of each cookie sculpture
7. bake 375° for 12 for 15 minutes, until lightly browned
8. transfer to cooling racks
9. decorate if desired when completely cooled

## VARIATIONS:

Confectioners Icing —
1. stir 2 cups confectioners sugar and enough milk to make spreadable (about 3 T.)
2. tint with food coloring
3. spread on cooled cookies
4. add additional candies or dried fruits (also see page 113 for Flow Icing)

## HINTS:

1. think of holiday ideas such as owls, cats, bells, stars, eggs, bunnies, hearts, flowers
2. remember that free form designs are wonderful

# ROLL SCULPTURE DOUGH

*good, easy recipe —*
*makes about forty 2″ sculptures*

## MATERIALS:
**cream —**
½ cup white or brown sugar
½ cup butter
**beat in —**
2 eggs
2½ to 2¾ cups flour
2 t. baking powder
1 t. vanilla

## PROCESS:
1. mix dough
2. chill dough 3 to 4 hours
3. roll and cut sculptures or free forms
4. bake at 375° for 7 to 12 minutes

## VARIATIONS:
1. decorate with icing when cool
2. decorate with candies, raisins, etc. before baking
3. paint with egg white mixed with food coloring to decorate before baking

# RICH ROLL SCULPTURES

*so good they may never make it to the oven —*
*makes about sixty 2″ sculptures*

**MATERIALS:**
bowl
spoon
cookie sheet
**cream —**
1 cup butter
⅔ cups sugar
**beat in —**
1 egg
**mix together and add —**
2⅓ cups flour, sifted
½ t. salt
1 t. vanilla

**PROCESS:**
1. make dough
2. chill 3 to 4 hours
3. roll out and cut, or mold with hands into free forms
   *hints:* best to pull parts from a ball than trying to stick
   parts on, although both will work
4. bake 8 to 10 minutes at 350°
5. cool
6. decorate if desired as in Roll Sculptures (page 102)

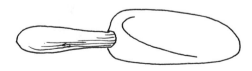

# PRETZEL DOUGH

*a warm, delicious yeast dough experience*

## MATERIALS:
1 pkg. yeast
1½ cups warm water
1 t. salt
1 T. sugar
4 cups flour
1 egg, beaten
salt (optional)

large bowl
spoon
cookie sheet
brush

## PROCESS:
1. measure warm water into large bowl
2. sprinkle on yeast and stir until soft
3. add salt, sugar, flour
4. mix and knead dough with hands
5. roll and twist into any desired shapes
6. place on greased cookie sheet
7. brush with beaten egg
8. sprinkle with salt (optional)
9. bake 12 to 15 minutes at 350°

# DOGGIE BISCUITS

*for people and dogs — makes 11½ dozen 3"x ¾" biscuits,
or a variety of other shapes*

## MATERIALS:

large bowl
small bowl
rolling pin
3½ cups flour
2 cups rye flour
1 cup corn meal
2 cups cracked wheat

½ cup instant nonfat
  dry milk (dry)
4 t. salt
1 envelope active dry yeast
¼ cup very warm water
2 to 3 cups chicken broth or other liquid
1 large egg, beaten with 1 T. milk

cookie sheets

## PROCESS:

1. mix flours, cracked wheat, corn meal, dry milk and salt in large bowl
2. sprinkle yeast over warm water and stir in small bowl
3. add yeast and 2 cups of broth to dry ingredients
4. mix well with hands
   *hint:* dough will be *very* stiff
5. if necessary, add a little more broth
6. roll out dough on floured surface to ¼" thickness and cut into desired shapes or squeeze dough into shapes
7. place on ungreased sheets
8. brush with egg-milk mixture
9. bake 45 minutes at 300°
10. turn off oven and leave in oven overnight

## VARIATIONS:

1. used canned broth or broth made from chicken flavor bouillon cubes
2. substitute water left over from cooking vegetables
3. make valentines for your dog
4. make decorations for a pet Christmas tree or holiday branch
5. wrap as gifts for your special friend (canine)

# PÂTÉ BRISÉE

*buttery and delicious when baked —*
*makes one 9″ crust or many smaller sculptures*

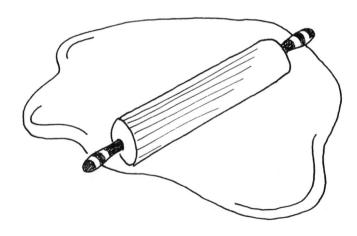

## MATERIALS:
1⅓ cups flour
¼ pound cold butter, cut 6 to 8 pieces
1 t. salt
2 to 3 T. ice water
food processor

## PROCESS:
1. place metal blade in food processor
2. add ingredients, except water
3. process until coarse meal
4. add water with machine running until dough forms a ball
5. refrigerate at least 30 minutes
6. model or roll and cut dough
7. bake unil golden at 350°
8. cool
   *hint:* Pate Brisee stores for months in the freezer, or two days in the refrigerator

## VARIATIONS:
1. decorate with raisins, candies, or chocolate chips before baking
2. see Pie Crust
3. make dough by hand

# PÂTÉ BRISÉE SUCRÉE

*pliable rich dough — stores for months in freezer,*
*2 days in refrigerator*

**MATERIALS:**
1¼ cups flour
¼ pound cold butter, cut in 6 or 8 pieces
1 t. salt
1 T. ice water
1 egg
food processor

**PROCESS:**
1. place metal blade in processor
2. add first three ingredients
3. process until coarse meal
4. with machine running, add water and egg until dough
   forms a ball
5. chill at least 30 minutes
6. model, or roll and cut dough
7. bake at 350° until lightly brown
8. cool

**VARIATIONS:**
1. decorate before or after baking
2. brush with colored egg white for a glossy finish
3. make dough by hand

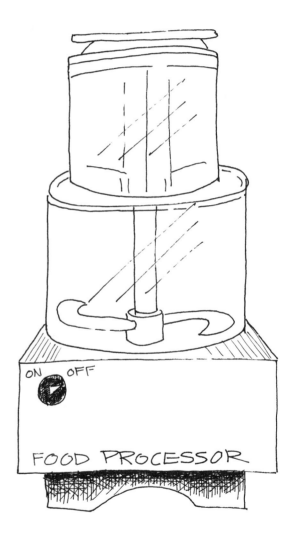

# PIECRUST

*better modeling quality than regular piecrust*

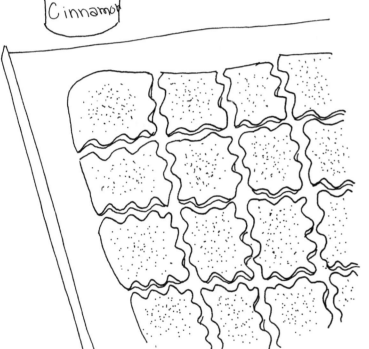

## MATERIALS:
1 cup flour
½ cup vegetable shortening
3 to 4 T. ice water
food processor

## PROCESS:

1. place metal blade in food processor
2. add flour and shortening and process until dough forms a ball
3. add water and continue processing until dough forms a ball
4. roll out and cut, or model flattened pieces as free form designs
5. bake at 350° until lightly brown

## VARIATIONS:
1. spread each piece with butter, and sprinkle with sugar and cinnamon before baking
2. paint with food coloring mixed with beaten egg before baking
3. make dough by hand

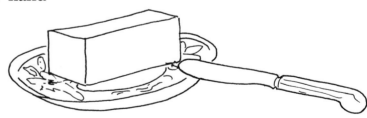

# GINGERBREAD MIX DOUGH

*spicy, easy modeling dough*

**MATERIALS:**
1 package gingerbread mix
¼ cup milk
¼ cup salad oil
bowl
plastic wrap
greased cookie sheet

**PROCESS:**
1. pour mix into large bowl
2. add milk, oil, and mix with hands or spoon
3. remove dough from bowl and shape into a ball
4. wrap with plastic and chill for 1 hour
5. roll dough ¼'' thick for cut-out sculptures or model individual balls of dough into free forms
6. place on greased cookie sheets, leaving room between
7. bake at 350° for 12 minutes
8. cool

**VARIATIONS:**
1. decorate if desired with icing and candies, raisins, etc.
2. poke a hole with a straw or toothpick before baking and hang with yarn when cool

# GINGERBREAD ARCHITECTURAL DOUGH

*suitable for building houses and other three dimensional projects — makes two 14"x 16"rectangles, ¼" thick, or many individual smaller projects*

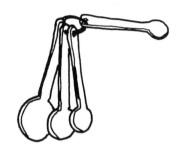

## MATERIALS:

bowl, spoon, plastic wrap, cookie sheets, cooling rack, board

**cream —**

1½ cups margarine or butter (3 sticks), or solid shortening
2½ cups granulated or brown sugar

**blend in —**

1½ t. salt
1½ t. baking soda
7 t. ground ginger
4 t. cinnamon

2 t. ground cloves
2 t. grated nutmeg
1 t. ground cardamom (optional)

**stir in —**

1½ cups molasses, dark or light
½ cup water

**add —**

4 cups flour, mix

**stir in —**

4 more cups flour, one cup at a time, and mix

## PROCESS:

1. make dough
2. divide in half, wrap, and chill or freeze
3. roll out dough on floured board, ¼" thick
4. cut patterns or freeforms
   *hint:* to make a house, cut rectangles of uniform size, remembering to cut windows, but leave them intact to remove after baking.
5. chill patterns on cookie sheet for 10 minutes in freezer or 15 minutes in refrigerator

**6.** bake 18 to 20 minutes for walls
10 minutes for freeform designs
at 350°
**7.** cool 1 minute
**8.** transfer to wire cooling rack
**9.** cool two hours or overnight

## VARIATIONS:

**light dough** for special effects
**1.** substitute light corn syrup or honey for molasses
**2.** dough will be a little stickier, so extra flour may be added
**dark dough** for special effects
**1.** use dark molasses and dark brown sugar
**2.** add extra ground cloves
**3.** bake longer

*fairly sophisticated process for young children, but can be accomplished successfully with adult help*

## MATERIALS:

jars or soup cans
architectural icing
architectural dough

spoon, spatula, or decorating tube
covered work area

## PROCESS:

1. if windows were cut, remove them now
2. stand the *back* wall and support with soup cans on either side
3. ice *back edge* of one *side* wall, and press to the back wall using another can for support
4. repeat other *side* wall
5. ice edges of *front* wall, and press into position, supporting the wall with soup cans
6. add additional icing for support
7. let dry overnight
8. remove cans
9. place on *roof* piece in position, and support edge with can
10. repeat for other *roof* piece
11. pipe icing across the peak of the roof
12. let dry 24 hours
13. decorate with more icing and assorted candy pieces

## VARIATIONS:

1. build gingerbread house on a pizza cardboard circle or on a pizza box covered with foil
2. ice and decorate the "yard" of the house
3. build chimney and fences from sugar cubes (paint these with food coloring and a brush)
4. add little wooden characters and ornaments for decoration
5. see variations for Architectural Icing

# ARCHITECTURAL ICING

*to use with Architectural Dough as an edible glue for building — has a hard finish*

## MATERIALS:

3 egg whites
½ t. cream of tartar
1 box powdered sugar sifted
½ t. lemon or orange
   extract, optional

bowl
mixer
spoon
food coloring
decorating tube
damp cloth

## PROCESS:

1. mix all ingredients on low speed
2. then 5 to 8 minutes on high speed, until peaks form with spoon
   *hint:* use grease-free utensils and bowl, otherwise icing will not peak
3. icing dries quickly, so keep covered with damp cloth while in use
4. fill decorating tube and assemble house or other project (or use a knife)

## VARIATIONS:

1. join graham cracker squares instead of gingerbread dough to build cracker houses
2. join any cookies (homemade or store bought) with architectural icing into sculptures of unknown design
3. join breadsticks for log cabin
4. join free form sculptures for a unique result

## FLOW OR COVERING ICING

1. add water until Architectural Icing is slightly thin
2. check consistency by dropping a bit from a spoon on icing
3. drop should blend in slowly
   *hint:* if it blends immediately, it is much too thin (add some sifted sugar, a tiny bit at a time)
4. use to fill in outlines and decorate
5. add food coloring if desired

# JOY GINGERBREAD

*perfect for gingerbread men —*
*makes eight 5" long/fat men, or 16 thinner ones*

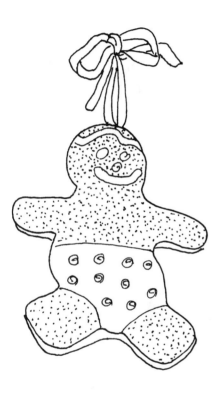

## MATERIALS:

**blend until creamy —**          bowl
¼ lb. butter                     greased cookie sheets
½ cup white or brown sugar    optional candies and raisins

**beat in —**
½ cup dark molasses

**sift —**
3½ cups flour

**resift with —**
1 t. soda                        ½ t. cinnamon
¼ t. cloves                      1 t. ginger
½ t. salt

add sifted ingredients to butter mixture with hands, adding
    ⅓ cup water for modeling activity
    or ¼ cup water for rolling and cutting activity

## PROCESS:

1. mix dough with hands
2. roll and model body parts, or make free form designs
3. stick them together on a greased pan
   *hint:* be sure to overlap and press parts together carefully
4. decorate before baking if desired with any of the following:
   redhots, raisins, candied cherries, chocolate chips, sprinkles, any candy bits
5. bake 8 minutes at 350°, or longer for thicker sculptures
6. test for doneness by pressing dough with finger
   *hint:* if it springs back, sculptures are ready to cool
7. cool

## VARIATIONS:

1. further decorate with:
   ½ cup powdered sugar
   few drops of water
   may add a drop or two food coloring
   apply icing with toothpick or small knife
2. use a cake decorating tube filled with icing
3. see Flow Icing (page 113)

# STAINED GLASS DOUGH

*fairly involved — makes about ten large colorful projects*

## MATERIALS:

1¾ cups whole wheat flour
1 cup all-purpose flour
1 t. pumpkin pie spice
¼ t. salt
½ t. baking soda

½ cup margarine or butter
1 cup packed brown sugar
1 egg
½ t. vanilla
½ cup dairy sour cream

3 ounces yellow or red clear
  hard candy, crushed
bowl
mixer
foil covered baking sheet
board

## PROCESS:

1. combine flours, spice, baking soda, and salt
2. in bowl, beat margarine on medium or until softened (CAUTION)
3. add sugar and beat until fluffy
4. add vanilla and egg and beat
5. add flour mixture and sour cream alternately, beating well
6. halve dough, cover, and chill 2 hours
7. on floured board, roll half of the dough ⅛'' thick
8. cut out any shapes up to 6-8''
    *hint:* add smaller shapes for decorations such as noses,
          eyebrows, leaves, etc. from scraps (applique)
    *hint:* cut out holes and fill with crushed hard candy
9. bake 6 to 8 minutes at 350° until edges are brown
10. cool on sheet 10 minutes
11. peel off foil, cool
12. store in airtight container or eat
    *hint:* makes about 10 large cookie sculptures

## VARIATIONS:

1. make stained glass windows
    *hint:* be careful not to make dough areas too narrow
2. make jack-o-lanterns, holiday ornaments, funny clown faces
3. frost if desired

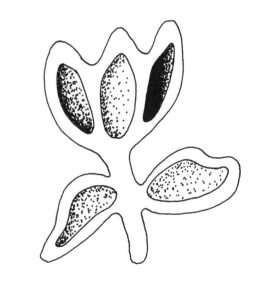

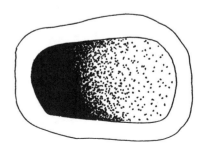

# PEANUT SYRUP DOUGH

*simple ingredients*

## MATERIALS:
1 cup peanut butter
1 cup corn syrup
1½ cups powdered sugar
1½ cups powdered milk
bowl
spoon

## PROCESS:
1. mix ingredients in bowl with spoon
2. more powdered milk may be needed to make dough
3. knead and shape

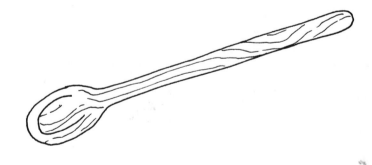

# PEANUT BUTTER PLAY DOUGH

*best edible dough for very young artists*

**MATERIALS:**

½ cup peanut butter    or...    1 part peanut butter
½ cup non-fat dry milk         1 part non-fat dry milk
⅔ T. honey, optional         1 T. honey per cup, optional

**PROCESS:**

1. mix equal parts of peanut butter and dry milk
2. add honey, optional
3. knead and mix until a good dough-like consistency
4. model and experiment as any playdough

**HINTS:**

1. keeps well in covered container in refrigerator
2. edible
3. does not harden well

# FROSTING DOUGH

*a sweet, easy favorite dough*

**MATERIALS:**
1 can frosting mix
1½ cups powdered sugar
1 cup peanut butter
spoon
bowl

**PROCESS:**
1. mix all ingredients in bowl with spoon
2. knead into workable dough
3. model as with any dough

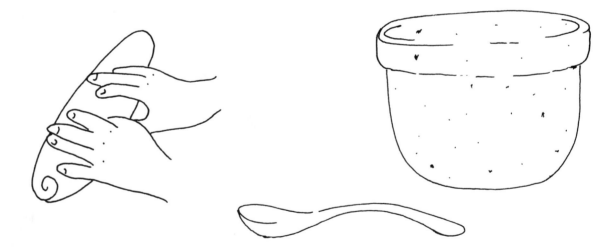

# MASHED POTATOES

*who can resist a volcano?*

**MATERIALS:**
peeler
potatoes
pot
masher
knife

**PROCESS:**
1. peel and dice potatoes with knife
2. cook over medium heat in pot until soft
3. drain
4. mash vigorously
5. model and explore mashed potatoes

**VARIATIONS:**
1. edible art — add other edible items such as ground cooked hamburger, slices of carrots, pieces of cheese, slices of green onions
2. add a liquid to a sculpture designed for flowing liquid (the volcano?)
3. drop food coloring into small piles and squish and mix colors

# YUMMY DOUGH

*a sweet, pliable dough — can be sticky*

**MATERIALS:**
½ cup brown sugar
¼ cup peanut butter
1 T. granola (optional)
bowl

**PROCESS:**
1. measure brown sugar and peanut butter into bowl
2. squeeze with hands
   *hint:* if sticky, add brown sugar
         if dry, add peanut butter
3. add granola, optional
4. explore dough freely

# MODELING MIXTURES & MORE

chapter 6

From Mudworks to Clay Modeling, the variety of the following unusual modeling compounds will delight all ages. Can you really make putty from toothpaste? Did you ever want to make a sand castle that you could keep? As you explore the 20 art experiences in Chapter 6, feel free to experiment with ingredients and results.

# MUDWORKS

*messy but basic art experience*

**MATERIALS:**

mud                       bucket or hose
  (dirt and water)       hands
outdoor work area        spade or shovel

**PROCESS:**

1. find an area in the yard or playground that is good dirt with few rocks, sticks, and leaves
   *hint:* garden areas are good
2. loosen an area with a shovel or spade suitable for working about 3 x 3 ft.
3. add water from a hose or bucket if too dry
4. mix with hands and spade or other tools
5. enjoy creating mudpies, patties, and other shapes
6. dry on cookie sheets, plywood, or other surface

*cleanup:* rinse heavy mud with hose, then wash with soap and water in sink

**VARIATIONS:**

1. bring clean dirt indoors in a plastic laundry tub, then add water until claylike, and create and explore
2. fill sand-table with dirt, then add water and explore
3. decorate with "sugar" (sand), chopped grass, crushed leaves, or pebbles

*cleanup:* loosen heavy mud from hands and arms in bucket of warm water, then wash with soap and water at sink as usual

# SANDWORKS

*inexpensive, wonderful art experience*

**MATERIALS:**
sand
water
bucket or hose
work area

**PROCESS:**
1. visit the beach or river shore
2. find wet sand
   *hint:* if tide is in, add water to an area of dry sand and
   mix with hands until sand holds together somewhat
3. explore and create

**VARIATIONS:**
1. add buckets, containers, and other tools to build shapes
   and scratch designs
2. work indoors in a large tub or sand table
3. build a castle
4. sculpt animals, creatures, or characters
5. sculpt anything, such as favorite toys, holiday symbols,
   maps, cars or boats, scenes, or stories

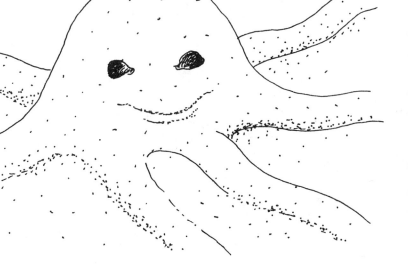

# SAND CASTLE

*basic building experience*

## MATERIALS:
scissors

colored construction paper

white glue

toothpicks

shoe box

molds such as:
 coffee can, funnel,
 pail, soup can

sand

## PROCESS:
1. using wet sand, fill the shoe box
2. turn upside down and carefully unmold
3. fill cans and do the same, and funnels, pails, etc.
4. glue paper triangles to toothpicks for flags and add to castle
5. make windows by poking holes carefully
6. experiment with imaginations

## VARIATIONS:
1. build surrounding landscape with ponds, trees, roads, and other ideas
2. add plastic toy animals, people, and boats or cars to scene

# SAND CASTLE KEEPER

*build a permanent sand castle*

**MATERIALS:**
6 cups sand
1 cup Paper Paste (see page 95)
water
containers: cans, plastic cups, tin can, small buckets,
          plastic toy pots, etc.
cardboard or plywood for background

**PROCESS:**
1. mix Paper Paste and sand
2. add water until claylike
   *hint:* should pack firmly into containers
3. start with large base and add smaller shapes
4. dry to permanent hardness

**VARIATIONS:**
1. cut windows and shapes with a spoon, knife, or other tools
2. carefully highlight areas with paint
3. see other ideas for Sand Castle

# NUTTY PUTTY

*make your own Silly Putty*

**MATERIALS:**
1 T. liquid starch
2 T. white glue
3 drops food coloring (optional)
plastic egg or screw top jar
bowl

**PROCESS:**
1. put starch in bowl
2. add glue and let set five minutes
3. if desired, add coloring
4. mix until starch is absorbed and color is spread smoothly
   *hint:* the more you mix, the better it gets
5. store in plastic egg or small jar overnight before using to pick up pictures from comics
6. use to bounce, pick up pictures from comics or newspaper, and mold into shapes

**HINTS:**
1. if left in open air, it will melt and then turn hard
2. add 1 t. more starch for a tougher, more rubbery putty
3. lasts several days if stored airtight
4. if putty dries out or gets tough, just dip into warm water and knead

# TOOTHPASTE PUTTY

*dries rock hard in 24 hours*

**MATERIALS:**
½ t. toothpaste (creamy, not gel)
1 t. white glue
2 t. cornstarch
½ t. water
small dish

**PROCESS:**
1. mix toothpaste, glue, and cornstarch in dish
2. mix with one finger
3. add water
4. mix until you have a lump of putty
   *hint:* putty should clean dish
5. wash and dry hands
6. squeeze and roll putty into ball
   *hint:* the more it's rolled, the better it gets
7. push, pull, roll and explore putty

**HINTS:**
1. putty begins to dry in 20 minutes, so to soften it, use a drop of water
2. toothpaste putty will dry rock hard in 24 hours

# PLASTIC JELLO

*can you tell it's artificial plastic?*

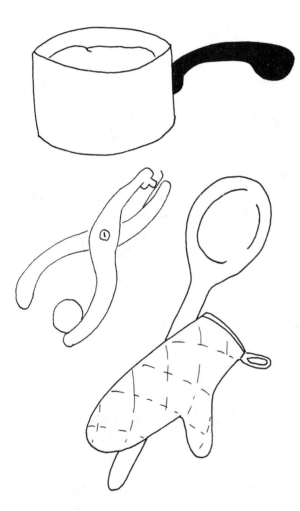

## MATERIALS:

1 envelope unflavored gelatin
3 T. water
few drops food coloring
saucepan and potholder

spoon
plastic coffee can lid, or
  other container lid
scissors, paper punch,
  needle, thread
  (optional)

## PROCESS:

1. in pan over medium heat, cook gelatin, water, and food coloring
2. stir constantly until dissolved
3. remove from heat
4. pour mixture into a coffee can lid
   *hint:* push any bubbles to the edge
5. let dry 1 to 2 days until hard
6. lift when edges are hard and sharp
7. cut with scissors to make a ring, a guitar pick, tiddlywinks, poker chips, or jewelry

## VARIATIONS:

1. to make sequins, punch out tiny rounds of plastic and string on thread
2. make doll's dishes
3. color with permanent pen to make stained glass
4. thread and hang in windows

# SIDEWALK CHALK

*works very well on sidewalks, but not on chalkboards*

**MATERIALS:**

6 eggshells
1 t. flour
1 t. very hot tap water

clean, smooth rock
2 dishes
spoon
strip of paper towel
sidewalk or playground

**PROCESS:**
1. wash and dry eggshells
2. grind them outside on clean, smooth concrete with a smooth rock
3. grind until you have a powder
4. sweep up powder with hands and put into a dish
5. pick out any big pieces of shell and throw them away
6. measure flour and hot water into another dish
7. add 1 T. of the eggshell powder
8. mix and mash until it sticks together
9. shape and press firmly into a chalk stick shape
10. roll stick up tight in strip of paper towel
11. dry for 3 days until rock hard
12. write with chalk (erase with shoe)

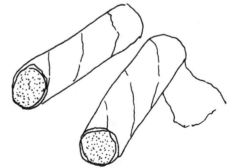

# SALT AND STARCH GOO

*grainy and gooey — piles and stacks*

**MATERIALS:**
½ cup liquid starch
2 cups rock salt
½ cup white glue
food coloring or tempera
spoons, bowls, cardboard

**PROCESS:**
1. mix starch with rock salt and white glue in bowl
2. add food coloring or tempera
   *hint:* grainy, gooey mixture
3. pile Goo onto a cardboard for three dimensional form
4. dries hard

# GOOP

*wonderful exploratory medium —
make small or large batches*

## MATERIALS:

one part cornstarch    or . . .    ½ cup cornstarch
one part water               ½ cup water
      food coloring or tempera, optional
      cookie sheets or trays, or large tub
      bowls, spoons

## PROCESS:

1. mix cornstarch with water, and optional color
2. pour mixture onto a tray, or make in a large tub
3. experience and enjoy this unique mixture's properties
4. keep reusing Goop

## VARIATIONS:

1. try adding more cornstarch and observe, experiment
2. try adding more water and observe, experiment
3. make Goop in a large water table as a group experience

# CARVING PASTE

*unique carving experience*

**MATERIALS:**
5 parts whiting (from hardware store)
1 part liquid glue
powdered tempera paint
water
bowl

**PROCESS:**
1. mix whiting, glue, and water in bowl until it looks like cream
2. add powdered tempera or other color
3. dry in a milk carton or other container

4. carve with any tools

**VARIATION:**
1. use to decorate ornaments, puppet heads, or plaques
2. substitute talcum powder or powdered chalk for whiting

# SOAP STONE CARVING

## MATERIALS:
4 T. very finely chopped hand soap
3 T. water
2 T. very finely chopped or grated crayon
knife
old pan

old spoon
wax paper
carving tools: nail
                 knife
                 hairpin, etc.

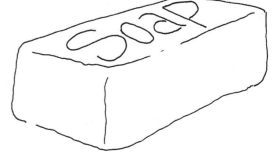

## PROCESS:
1. mix soap and water in a pan over low heat
   *hint:* if soap is perfumed, open a window
2. cook and stir until soap is melted and water is gone
3. add crayon gratings
4. cook and stir until they melt completely
5. scrape mixture onto wax paper and cool
   *hint:* clean pan and spoon right away
        (difficult to clean when cool)
6. press mixture into 2 or 3 stone shapes and balls
7. let dry 1 or 2 days
8. carve your soap stone with a small knife or other tool
   (nail, hairpin, screwdriver, etc.)

## VARIATIONS:
make —
1. make wax animals
2. jewels for a treasure chest
3. holiday shapes
4. boats
5. other shapes

# DETERGENT DOUGH

*dough is thick enough to pile up,
but not to model*

## MATERIALS:
1 cup detergent, powdered
⅛ cup water, plus food coloring
egg beater
bowl, spoon
cardboard, box, or bag

## PROCESS:
1. mix detergent with water
2. beat with egg beater until smooth, shiny, and stiff
3. stack and pile onto a base such as a box, a bag, or a piece of cardboard
4. make sculpture or explore as a playdough

# SOAP BALLS

**MATERIALS:**
2 cups Ivory Snow detergent
2 T. water
food coloring
bowl

**PROCESS:**
1. pour detergent in a bowl
2. add colored water gradually until soap forms a ball with hands
3. add more water if necessary
4. experiment with other shapes
5. use as soap

**VARIATION:**
1. makes a nice gift
2. use as soap at home
3. use as soap at school

# SOAPSUDS CLAY

*messy and amazing clay*

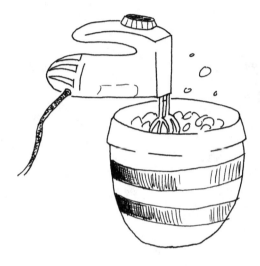

**MATERIALS:**
¾ cup soap powder such as Ivory Snow
1 T. warm water
electric mixer
large bowl

**PROCESS:**
1. mix soap and water in bowl
2. beat with mixer until claylike (CAUTION)
3. mold clay into objects
4. dries to hard finish

**HINTS:**
1. makes 1 cup
2. may be doubled or tripled

**VARIATIONS:**
**''Snow''**
1. beat 2 parts soap powder to 1 part water
2. spread like frosting on heavy cardboard
3. can be used to decorate cardboard holiday ornaments
   *hint:* dries to a rubbery, smooth surface overnight

# INDOOR SNOWMEN

*a favorite for all ages when it snows*

**MATERIALS:**
clean snow
plastic container or plate
container for snow, such as a bucket
mittens
small containers
strips of colorful fabric, trims, buttons, raisins,
   or other decorative items

**PROCESS:**
1. bring bucket of clean snow inside
2. wear mittens, if desired
3. build a two-snowball snowman in a plastic container or
   on a plate
4. decorate with a strip of material for a scarf if desired
5. add other decorations such as buttons

**VARIATIONS:**
1. build *any* snow creature or sculpture
2. decorate with collage type items:
   beans, seeds, sequins, feather, doll clothes, jewelry, beads,
   macaroni, pasta
3. spray snow with food coloring and water in a hand-held
   sprayer for a colorful effect
4. make snowman edible: use only food items, and possibly
   mix snow with vanilla and sugar before modeling
5. build outdoor, full size snowmen

*use caution with melting paraffin —*
*easy to carve*

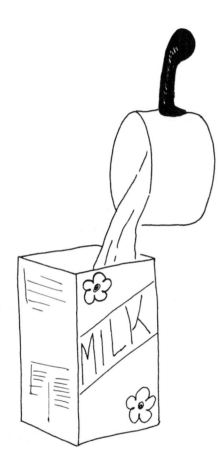

## MATERIALS:
paraffin
old double boiler or pan
container to use as a mold (milk carton, tin can, box)
carving tool (knife, stick, nail, hairpin)
optional color (wax crayons)

## PROCESS:

1. melt paraffin in double boiler over low heat
2. pour melted wax into mold and allow to cool and harden
3. dip mold in hot water until paraffin releases, or tear cardboard from paraffin
4. carve the block into any form

## VARIATIONS:
1. color can be added to the melted paraffin by mixing in waxed crayons
2. pour wax into a shallow container and carve a relief
3. use beeswax and do not melt (see Resource Guide)

# CRAYON MOLDS

## MATERIALS:
1 ounce paraffin or candle wax
can
1 t. linseed oil or turpentine
3 T. powdered paint pigment
paper towel tube or juice cans
WARNING: OMIT TURPENTINE WHEN
　　　　　MADE BY SMALL CHILDREN

## PROCESS:
1. cut up paraffin or wax in can
2. set in pan of water over low heat until melted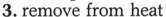
3. remove from heat
4. add powdered pigment
5. stir
6. pour mixture into a 3″ section of paper towel tube
7. when hardened, add rest of mixture
8. repeat for each color desired
9. when hard, tube is removed from entire crayon or tip only
10. draw as with any crayon

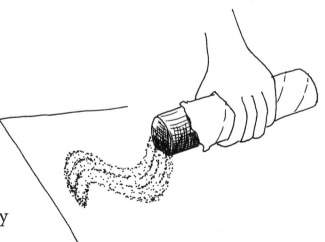

## VARIATIONS:
1. experiment with other mold shapes
2. for more crayon projects, see the book *Scribble Cookies* by MaryAnn F. Kohl
3. use Crayon Molds as you would any crayon

# CLAY MODELING BASIC EXPERIENCE

*there's nothing like the feel of real clay*

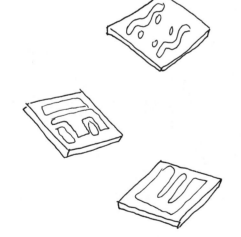

## MATERIALS:
commercial water base clay
work surface board or table covered with oil cloth

## PROCESS:
1. squeeze or push clay to form objects
2. work towards pulling parts rather than trying to stick them on
3. allow piece to dry at room temperature

## VARIATIONS:
1. use a modeling tool to carve away piece
2. roll coils and build a pot or bowl
3. roll clay flat and cut
4. cut square tiles and decorate

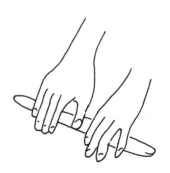

# MOIST CLAY

**MATERIALS:**
5 pounds clay from art or supply store
  (do not buy oil base clay)
newspaper, plastic, or oilcloth to cover table
wooden board, or cardboard to work on
plastic or other cloth to keep clay moist while not using
work clothes
optional:
  tools such as craft stick, rolling pin, knife, hairpin, hammer, blocks
paint for dry objects
to preserve: liquid wax, shellac, clear varnish, or colorless nail polish

**PROCESS:**
1. squeeze, roll, flatten, allowing for exploring
   *note:* always try to make a clay object from one piece so
          parts won't fall off when they dry
2. wet fingers and smooth clay, or brush damp sponge over it
3. allow piece to dry at room temperature

**TO FINISH:**
1. dry
2. dip in liquid wax, paint with shellac, vanish, spray with
   clear acrylic, or use nail polish

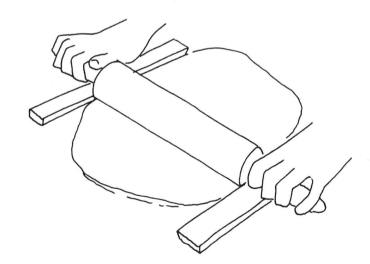

**TO FIRE:**
1. clay objects should dry slowly to prevent cracking
   *definition:* greenware
   *hint:* greenware may be wrapped with a damp cloth to
          slow the drying process

2. fire to a temperature of at least 1500° in a kiln
   *hint:* work with someone who is familiar with the kiln
   process
3. glaze can be applied to the fired-once clay
   *definition:* bisque
   *hint:* apply glaze with brush, spray, or by dipping
4. if no kiln is available, greenware can be finished by waxing, painting with enamel, shellac or varnish, or with tempera paint
   *hint:* if tempera paint is used, protect with plastic spray, varnish, or shellac

## HINTS:
1. moist clay may become moldy or rancid if kept too long while wet in a covered container
2. store in two plastic bags, one inside the other
3. store in cool place (galvanized garbage can helps)
4. if clay becomes too wet, spread it out to dry on an absorbent surface, such as a cloth covered board
5. if clay becomes too dry, break it up, smash it, and soak it in water for one or two days (pour off extra water and treat as clay which is too wet)

A SIMPLE BOX KILN

# RESOURCE GUIDE

# COMMERCIAL CLAY AND MODELING PRODUCTS

**ALGINATE IMPRESSION MATERIAL**
"Jeltrate"
ask your local orthodontist about how to order
this amazing molding compound
quick setting

**BEESWAX**
"Knet-Bienewachs"
for modeling like clay
comes in colors and natural
has a pleasant, natural honey scent
very pliable, unique, forgiving medium
does not dry out, can not be baked
> RUDUOLF STEINER COLLEGE
> attn: Bookstore
> 9200 Fair Oaks Blvd.
> Fair Oaks, CA 95628

**CAST-A-HAND**
for all ages, supervise younger children
non-toxic
includes 2 casts
add water to bucket
easy clean up
> KOPY KAST CORPORATION
> P.O. Box 3381
> Skokie, IL 60076

**CELLUCLAY**
non-toxic
needs no firing
mixes easily molds quickly

instant papier mache
good for figurines, jewelry, relief maps, models
available in 1, 5, 12 and 24 lb. bricks
> ACTIVIA PRODUCTS, INC.
> P.O. Box 1296
> Marshall, TX 75670-0023

**CLAYOLA**
1 lb. box
variety of colors,
one color per box
non-toxic
non-hardening
> BINNEY AND SMITH
> Easton, PA 18042

**CLAYTIME**
ages 3 and up
soft, pliable, non-toxic
comes with clay, molds, and tools
> PASTIME INDUSTRIES LIMITED
> 200 5th Ave.
> New York, NY

**DARWI**
1 lb.
modeling compound
ready to use
air dries
dampen as you use and smooth with wet finger
also available:
Darwi paints and varnish
> DARWI
> BOSDON-NELIS
> LIEGE-BELGIQUE

**DAS PRONTO AND TERRACOTTA**
2 lb. and other sizes
air hardening
let dry and decorate
paint or varnish
stores in plastic bag
available in dinosaur kit and beginning sculpting
set
> BATTAT INC.
> ADICA PONGO DIVSION
> 2 Industrial Blvd.
> West Circle, Plattsburg, NY 12901

**DENTAL WAX**
31 sheets
1 lb. box of 3" x 5" x 1/16" sheets
model and explore
> KNORR BEESWAX
> 14906 Via de la Valls
> Del Mar, CA 92014

**FIMO**
bright colors
modeling clay
harden in 275° oven
coat with Fimo Laquer when cool
dry

**FRIENDLY PLASTIC**
4.4 oz. colored pellets
hardens
can be remelted

use:
add pellets to boiling water
drain
shape with hands, press in mold, or
   use tools
hardens as it cools
decorate, use glitter or feathers while soft or paint
   when hard
can be remelted and reshaped
> FRIENDLY PLASTIC CO., LTD.
> Boulder, CO

**GALT NEWDAY MODELING SET**
tools and clay in a bucket

**GALT TOYS**
**INSTANT PAPIER MACHE SET**
ages 7+
mix adhesive
dries to hard finish
includes bowl, spoon, and tools
> JAMES GALT AND CO. LTD.
> Cheadle, Cheshire, England

**GRANNY'S DABBLIN DOUGH**
non-toxic
no odor
available in 20 colors
packed in 5 patty bucket (2.5 lb.)
primary assortment or florescent assortment
air dry several days or bake in 200° oven
may be painted when dry
> TREE HOUSE TOYS, INC.
> 4105 Pond Circle
> Bethelehem, PA 18017

**GRUMBACHER MOIST CLAY**
5 lbs.
comes ready to use
fires or air hardens
recommended for clay use with all ages
younger children, supervised
> M.GRUMBACHER, INC.
> 460 West 34th St.
> New York, NY 10001

**HARBUTT'S PLASTICINE**
comes in 4+ colors
non-toxic
good for ages above 3
comes in several sets:
   bears, farm, cookie cutter
> PETER PAN PLAYTHINGS
> Bretton Way Ltd.
> Bretton, Peterborough
> England PE38YA

**KEMPER TOOLS**
PTK POTTERY TOOL KIT
8 tools
potters rib, steel scraper, wood modeling tool,
needle tool, ribbon tools, loop tool, sponge, wire
clay cutter
> KEMPER MFG INC.
> P.O. 696
> Chino, CA 91710

**KLEAN KLAY**
non-toxic modeling clay
9½ oz.  12 oz.

**LEISURE CLAY** by PLASTALINA
comes in many nice colors
including metallic gold
non-toxic
non-hardening
5 lbs. of one color
16 oz.-5 pieces, assorted or one color
> LEISURECRAFTS COMPANY
> Los Angeles, CA 90221

**LITE-TUFY**
60 grams
plaster hardener
add directly to plaster powder
surprisingly light weight
chalk free
chip resistant
for best results, dry in a warm place
    such as a mild oven, just hot to the touch

**MAKO MOULAGES**
for molding and decorating
ages 6-13
plaster, brush, paints
> MEUX NATHAN S.A.
> Paris, France

**MARZIPAN**
edible candylike dough
from baking or grocery departments

**MIX-A-MOLD**
non-toxic
non-flammable
odorless
comes in 8 oz. or 2½ lb.
mix water with product
forms a rubbery, flexible mold in minutes
pour into mold container
set, remove object
mold is now ready to cast
> RUB IN BUFF
> Division of American Art Clay Co.
> Box 68163
> Indianapolis, Indiana 46268

**MOLD IT**
1 pt.
pure liquid rubbery latex
for making detailed molds, masks, dolls
pour into rubber or plaster mold
dry in 140° oven 1 hour
> JOLI PLASTICS AND CHEMICAL
> CORPORATION
> 14922 Garfield Ave.
> Paramount, CA 90723

**NEVO.350**
2 lb.
an oven firing clay
or air dry
waterproof without glazing
keeps moist in plastic bag
use: air dry or place on baking sheet in cool oven
set at 350° for one hour
cool
use or decorate
> AMERICAN ART CLAY
> Indianapolis, IN 46222

**PERMASTONE**
3 lbs. or 14 oz.
extra strong casting medium
add 3 parts Permastone to 1 part water
use like plaster
releases from a mold in 20-30 minutes
dry overnight before painting
> ACTIVA
> 582 Market St.
> San Francisco, CA 94101

**PLASTER OF PARIS**
5 lb. bag
package directions:
measure 2 parts plaster to 1 part water
add all to container
let it soak a few moments
then stir
pour plaster into mold
shake to level and release bubbles
set or cure 30-50 minutes
remove
trim edges
dry thoroughly
then stain, paint or gild
*DO NOT WASH PLASTER DOWN THE SINK OR DRAIN*

**PLAY DOH**
non-toxic
not a clay
comes in many kits:
Mop Top Hair Shop
Mask
Gadgets
Fingles
Pocket Knife
and more
> PLAY DOUGH
> by Kenner Parker Toy Co.
> Cincinnati, Ohio 45202

**PONGO**
modeling dough
non-hardening
washable

**DIDO**
by Pongo
soft modeling dough
non-stain
non-toxic
> BATTAT INC.
> Adica Pongo Division
> 2 Industrial Blvd.
> West Circle
> Plattsburg, NY 12901
> made in Italy

**POTTERY CRAFT WHEEL**
ages 8 +
air dry clay
non-toxic
includes paints and glaze
needs two D cell batteries
> IDEAL INC.
> Portland, OR 97207

**POUR AND PAINT**
molding set
5 +
non-toxic
ready to paint in 45 minutes
no oven
> EASY ART INC.
> 2103 W. 10th
> Eugene, OR 97402

**PRO ART TOOL SET**
8 modeling and clay tools
    (see Kemper Tools)

**ROMA PLASTILINA**
modeling compound
2 lbs.
comes in four consistencies:
no. 1 — soft, extremely plastic
no. 2 — medium, general work
no. 3 — medium firm, for smaller models
no. 4 — very hard, for small figures, medallions,
    reliefs
will never harden, crust, or deteriorate
improves with use and age
> JOLLY KING
> 38 East 30th St.
> New York, NY 10016

**ROSEART PLAY CLAY**
non-toxic
non-hardening
> ROSE ART INDUSTRIES, INC.
> Bloomfield, NY 07003

## SCULPEY
2 lbs.
modeling compound
knead until soft and shape
bake at 300° 15-30 minutes
cool
paint with acrylics
otherwise, is white

can be sanded, carved
won't shrink

## SUPER SCULPEY
1 lb. ceramic-like
bakes hard in oven
can be carved, sanded, drilled
can add more to a baked piece and bake again
knead, shape, bake at 300° 15-20 minutes
cool
paint

## SCULPEY III
comes in ten bright, individually wrapped colors
2 oz.
same directions as regular Sculpey

## SCULPEY MODELING TOOLS
fiberglass tools
4 tools, 1 brush
POLYFORM PRODUCTS, INC.
9420 Byron Street
Schiller Park, IL 60176

## TYCO SUPER DOUGH
many colors, and sets
ex. Snackshop
Flower Making Basket
Squeezers
TYCO INDUSTRIES, INC.
Moorestown, NJ 08057
1-800-257-7728

*note:*
Many other products are available for modeling and molding. Check your local toy, hobby, art, and hardware stores. Another excellent resource is school and art supply catalogs. If you find a product you especially like, please write to Bright Ring Publishing and share your findings.

# WHERE TO FIND

**commercial clays and modeling compounds**
hobby, art, and craft stores
toy stores
craft dept.

**cream of tartar**
**alum**
grocery store

**decorating tubes**
cake decorating store
variety store, kitchen dept.
kitchen store

**dextrin**
1. from chemistry or science teachers
2. All-World Scientific and Chemical, Seattle,
   1-800-206-282-2133
3. order from your pharmacy

**food processor**
variety store, kitchen dept.
kitchen store

**funnel**
car part store
kitchen store

**garlic press**
grocery store
kitchen store

**Gesso**
art and hobby stores

**glazes**
all at hardware stores, art and hobby stores
   shellac
   varnish
   clear acrylic spray
   clear glaze
   clear enamel spray

**glycerine**
school supply stores
pharmacy

**liquid starch**
grocery store, soap section
school supply stores
art stores

**oil of cinnamon**
**oil of cloves**
pharmacy
grocery store

**paraffin**
grocery store, canning department

**plaster of paris**
hardware store
hobby and craft stores

**popsicle sticks**
craft and hobby store

**putty**
hardware store

**rock salt**
variety store
grocery store
gardening store

**sand**
hardware store
beach
desert

**sawdust**
lumber yard
shop class

**spackle**
hardware store

**vermiculite**
gardening store
gardening department or variety store

**water base clay (Moist Clay)**
hobby store
art supply store

**wheat paste**
wallpaper store
hobby store
make it at home

**whiting**
hardware store

**zonalite**
lumber yard
hardware store

# BIBLIOGRAPHY

Becker, Marion Rombauer and Rombauer, Irma. JOY OF COOKING. New York:
    New American Library, 1973.         ISBN 0-452-25425-6

Braasch, Barbara. SUNSET CHILDREN'S CRAFTS. Menlo Park, CA: Lane
    Publishing Co., 1976.         ISBN 0-376-04124-2

Clark, David E. SUNSET COOKIES. Menlo Park, CA: Lane Publishing Co., 1985.
        ISBN 0-376-02387-2

DiValentin, Maria. PRACTICAL ENCYCLOPEDIA OF CRAFTS. New York:
    Sterling Publishing Co., Inc., 1970.         ISBN 0-8069-5150-8

Fiarotta, Phyllis. SNIPS AND SNAILS AND WALNUT WHALES. New York:
    Workman Publishing, 1975.         ISBN 0-911104-75-5

Garritson, Jane. CHILD ARTS. Menlo Park, CA: Addison Westley Publishing
    Company, 1979.         ISBN 0-201-02874-3

Leeming, Joseph. FUN WITH CLAY. New York: Lippincott Company, 1944.

Johnson, Jann. SWEET DREAMS OF GINGERBREAD. New York: 1986.
        ISBN 0-02-496780-7

Kane, Jane. ART THROUGH NATURE. Holmes Beach, FL: Learning Publications,
    Inc., 1956.         ISBN 0-918452-44-9

Kern, Marna Elyea. BREADCRAFT. Boston: Houton Mifflin Company, 1977.
        ISBN 0-395-25770-0

Kohl, MaryAnn F. SCRIBBLE COOKIES and Other Independent Creative Art
    Experiences for Children. Bellingham, WA: Bright Ring Publishing, 1985.
        ISBN-0-935607-10-2

Meilach, Dona A. CREATING WITH PLASTER. Chicago: Reilly and Lee Company,
    1966.

Peattie, Charles. PAPIER-MACHE. East Sussex, England: Wayland Publishers,
    1977.         ISBN-85340-501-8

Price, Lowi and Wronksy, Marilyn. CONCOCTIONS. New York: E.P. Dutton and
    Company Inc., 1976.         ISBN 0-525-28137-1

Reingold, C.B. CUISINART FOOD PROCESSOR COOKING. New York: Dell
    Publishing, 1981.         ISBN 0-440-51585-8

Sattler, Helen Roney. RECIPES FOR ART AND CRAFT MATERIALS. New York:
    Lothrop, Lee and Sherpard Books, 1973.         ISBN 0-688-07374-3

Stangl, Jean. MAGIC MIXTURES. Belmont, CA: Fearon Teacher Aids, 1986.
        ISBN 0-8224-4377-5

Wirtenberg, Patricia Z. ALL-AROUND-THE-HOUSE ART AND CRAFT BOOK.
    Menlo Park, CA: Lane Publishing Co., 1976.

# MATERIALS INDEX

# MATERIALS INDEX (continued)

# PROJECT INDEX

## ABOUT THE AUTHOR

MaryAnn's interest in creative art for children comes from her years of teaching elementary age children in the Pacific Northwest, using language experience and learning center teaching methods. More recently she has worked with children throughout Washington as an educational consultant in the areas of art, illustrating, and publishing for young authors. In addition to writing and teaching, MaryAnn enjoys skiing, watching wildlife on the lake, and being a mom. MaryAnn lives in Bellingham, Washington with her husband and two daughters.

# BRIGHT IDEAS BOOKSHELF

**Good Earth Art** — Environmental Art For Kids
MaryAnn F. Kohl, Cindy Gainer

*11 x 8½ • 224 pages • $16.95 • paper*
*ISBN 0-935607-01-3*

*"Over 200 projects to keep inquisitive minds exploring art for years... with materials as close as your garden or the burrs on your sweater."*
Lynn Johnston, cartoonist, *For Better or For Worse*

*"...a wonderful resource filled with simple ideas to help children create and recycle — an innovative connection between art and science."*
Inky Kim, librarian, Science Access Center, New York Hall of Science

*"Preschoolers, art teachers, adventurous parents, and anyone who likes to play in mud, playdough, papier-mache and similar mediums will be ecstatic over Kohl's book. Ideal for fun or serious art. Basic, enormously useful text. A treasure trove of projects and ideas."*
American Library Association *Booklist*
★ *Starred Review* ★

**MUDWORKS** — Creative Clay, Dough, and Modeling Experiences
MaryAnn F. Kohl
Illustrations Kathleen Kerr

*11 x 8½ • 152 pages • $14.95 • paper*
*ISBN 0-935607-02-1*

**Scribble COOKIES** — And Other INDEPENDENT CREATIVE Art Experiences for Children
NEW EDITION
MaryAnn F. Kohl

*11 x 8½ • 144 pages • $12.95 • paper*
*ISBN 0-935607-10-2*

*"Scribble Cookies stresses the importance of individual creative exploration in a safe, non-competitive, open-ended environment. Activities need only basic art supplies and common kitchen materials. Highly recommended."*
Canadian Society for Education Through Art

---

# ORDER FORM

*NOTE: 10% discount for orders of 4 or more books.

Bright Ring Publishing

P.O. Box 5768
Bellingham, WA 98227
(206) 734-1601 / Fax (206) 676-1271

Name: _____

Address: _____

_____

Phone: _____ Zip: _____

| Quantity | Title of Book | Price |
|---|---|---|
|  |  |  |
|  |  |  |
|  |  |  |
|  |  |  |

**SHIPPING CHART**
USPS Book Rate, 4th Class:
   $2.00 — 1st book
   $1.00 — each additional

UPS:
   Add $1.50/book to *USPS rate*

AIR MAIL:
   Add $3.00/book

| | |
|---|---|
| Total for books | |
| Deduct 10% for orders of 4 or more books. | |
| *SUBTOTAL* | |
| Sales Tax @ 7.8% (Washington only) | |
| Shipping (see chart) | |
| **TOTAL ENCLOSED** | |

*Please make checks payable to:*
*Bright Ring Publishing*

**GOOD EARTH ART**
Environmental Art for Kids........................................ $16.95

**MUDWORKS**
Creative Clay, Dough, and Modeling Experiences.................. $14.95

**SCRIBBLE COOKIES**
and Other Independent Creative Art
Experiences for Children .......................................... $12.95

*Orders shipped within 3 business days. Allow 2 weeks for shipment to arrive.*